Techniques of
CLOSE
READING

For Jackie Savoy, Terry Olliver, and all my Port Arthur friends, new and old, silver and gold.

Techniques of
CLOSE
READING

Barry Brummett

The University of Texas at Austin

Los Angeles | London | New Delhi
Singapore | Washington DC

For information:

SAGE Publications, Inc.
2455 Teller Road
Thousand Oaks,
   California 91320
E-mail: order@sagepub.com

SAGE Publications India Pvt. Ltd.
B 1/I 1 Mohan Cooperative
   Industrial Area
Mathura Road, New Delhi 110 044
India

SAGE Publications Ltd.
1 Oliver's Yard
55 City Road
London EC1Y 1SP
United Kingdom

SAGE Publications Asia-Pacific
   Pte. Ltd.
33 Pekin Street #02-01
Far East Square
Singapore 048763

Printed in the United States of America

Library of Congress Cataloging-in-Publication Data

Brummett, Barry, 1951-
Techniques of close reading/Barry Brummett.
    p. cm.
Includes bibliographical references and index.
ISBN 978-1-4129-7265-9 (pbk.)
   1. Rhetoric—Social aspects. I. Title.

P301.5.S63B78 2010
808—dc22   2009018026

This book is printed on acid-free paper.

           12   13   10   9   8   7   6   5   4   3

Acquisitions Editor:	Todd R. Armstrong
Editorial Assistant:	Aja Baker
Production Editor:	Astrid Virding
Copy Editor:	April Wells-Hayes
Typesetter:	C&M Digitals (P) Ltd.
Proofreader:	Dennis W. Webb
Cover Designer:	Gail Buschman
Marketing Manager:	Jennifer Reed Banando

Brief Contents

Detailed Contents

Preface

This is a "how to" book designed largely for use in college classes. It teaches students how to *see* what is in a text. Therefore, in a sense it is a book on mindfulness and noticing. I hope that you, the instructor of these courses, find it useful.

Most other textbooks of this sort directly address critical analysis. Such books may be used in courses of rhetorical or media criticism, popular culture, and so forth. Typically, these books review different kinds of methods and theories, covering Marxist, deconstructionist, feminist, and related approaches to understanding texts. I have written just such a book myself, *Rhetoric in Popular Culture*.

What I felt was missing from many of these otherwise fine books (and, in fact, from my own) was an approach that addressed very basic techniques of looking at a text and noticing what was there. At the same time, such an approach cannot be divorced from a concern for theory and method. Students who are grappling with a text need help, and they also need a way to connect the techniques they are learning with the larger issues of theory and method.

In this book I have tried to develop a set of techniques that can be used across many theories and techniques. Of course, there are limits to any such an array of techniques, but my hope is that regardless of the theoretical or methodological stance being taught, students may find a selection of techniques in this book to help them connect theory and method to actual texts. In Chapter 1, I hail the student as a reader and a critic of texts. This chapter explains what it is to read a text and critique it. Students are encouraged to think of the many contexts in their own lives in which they can perform and then share a critical close reading.

In Chapter 2, I develop a rationale for the relationships among theory, method, and technique. This discussion may facilitate a discussion on theory and method in their own right and so may serve purposes beyond the actual examination of texts. The chapter examines deductively the relationships of theories, methods, and texts, although an inductive approach growing out of familiarity with techniques is then invited. Chapter 2 also explains the ethical stances and risks associated with critique and with attending to critique.

Chapter 3 explains the technique of examining form in a critical close reading. Such dimensions of narrative as coherence and sequence, tensions and resolution, alignment and opposition are explored. Techniques are discussed for noticing genre and personae and for teasing out the political implications of form.

Chapter 4 is keyed to Kenneth Burke's scheme of four master tropes. The chapter shows how attention to tropes—specifically metaphor, metonymy, synecdoche, and irony—can reveal dimensions of a text that may not otherwise be noticed. Students are taught to develop sensitivity to the ways in which language can encode complex meanings.

Chapter 5 studies the idea of argument and offers techniques for identifying ideologies in argument. *Ideology* is surely one of the most theory-dependent terms in use today, but I avoid the specific or exclusive use of any one theory. A major feature of this chapter is an extended discussion of three sample texts that span quite a range of history and type.

The Conclusion is a single extended reading of a comic strip that appeared shortly before the inauguration of Barack Obama as president. It would run counter to the advice I give in the book and would seem far too mechanical to try to use all the covered techniques in that final close reading. Rather, a selection of some techniques from each chapter shows students how different techniques may be used together.

The book is by intention short. This is so that it can be paired with a longer, theoretically and methodologically more developed book. If the course you teach is short, however, this book could work as a stand-alone text if supplemented with your own material. I have not explained any technique exhaustively but instead have tried to provide a launching pad for your own creative teaching. I wish you all success in your teaching and would enjoy hearing from you how the book works in your class.

❖ ACKNOWLEDGMENTS

I want to thank Todd Armstrong of SAGE for his ongoing support of several of my writing projects. He is a great editor. Thanks to the reviewers of the manuscript who were so helpful. Thanks to the faculty and students of the Department of Communication Studies at The University of Texas at Austin, a community of excellence.

The following reviewers are gratefully acknowledged:

Lisa Bailey, University of South Carolina, Department of English; A. Robin Bowers, Plymouth State University, Department of English; A. J. Grant, Robert Morris University, Department of English Studies and Communication Skills; Diane Keeling, University of Colorado at Boulder, Department of Communication; Thomas K. Nakayama, Northeastern University, Department of Communication Studies; Roy Schwartzman, University of North Carolina at Greensboro, Department of Communication Studies; and Mary E. Triece, The University of Akron, School of Communication.

1

On Noticing
What You See and Hear

❖ ❖ ❖

Recently, I went to an amusement park outside of San Antonio, down the road from where I live. Take a look at this photograph of a sign near the entrance to a particularly scary roller coaster.

It's the kind of thing you might glance at and not give a second thought to, but take a harder look. Consider the context: San Antonio, one of the ten largest cities in the United States, is also a city in which the majority of people are of Latino, Hispanic, or Spanish-speaking heritage. So why is the warning sign in Spanish smaller than the one in English? Perhaps of more interest is the question of what that difference does to people who see it. Think about what message size conveys all by itself.

As I write this, I am in Cape Town, South Africa, for a conference. The conference organizer left me this note when I arrived: "Welcome! I hope your travels were pleasant. As you get settled, give me a call on 082 731 xxxx. I am just around the corner, and perhaps we can meet up for a coffee on Tuesday or Wednesday."

It's a perfectly fine note, but it contains a couple of words that I would not have used had I written it. He asks me to call him "on" such and such a number. I would have asked someone to call me "at" a given number. And he wants to have "a coffee." I would have said

Figure 1.1

To view this image in full resolution, please visit www.sagepub.com/brummettstudy.

"coffee." Not a big deal, but it's interesting to me. I don't know that much about this person. He teaches at a large midwestern university in the United States, as have I most of my life, but I don't know if he's *from* the Midwest. So I'm wondering what the source of our minor language differences would be. As a frequent traveler to South Africa, has he adopted a South African, British, or European way of speaking? Or does his usage reflect some other pattern? What do my preferred wordings say about me? Not the most earth-shaking questions, but their answers reveal some interesting things about where he and I are from and what our social allegiances are.

Most people wouldn't even notice this wording, and you might be wondering why I would do so. And you might not have paid much attention to the signs in front of the roller coaster in our first example. But I think that being in the habit of noticing what people say and write and being able to reflect on what these messages mean is a useful habit to pick up. It is a habit of *close reading,* and this is a book about how to train yourself to be a good close reader. In Chapter 1, I argue that *close reading is the mindful, disciplined reading of an object with a view to deeper understanding of its meanings.* The objects we will learn to read closely are texts or messages. It's important to be able to read closely because it helps us to see things about messages, such as the difference in size of the warning signs, that *do* make a difference and do affect how people think.

These two examples—the roller coaster sign and my colleague's note—show us two dimensions in which close reading is important. First, it is important *socially.* As citizens, as people active in public life, we need to know how the messages we encounter may influence the public in important ways. We all know that instances of racism and ethnic inequality occur from time to time, for example. Rarely will we find these and other problems openly and explicitly expressed or perpetuated. Instead, we are more likely to be socially influenced in small ways—such as through signs in an amusement park. A single sign in an amusement park that makes English bigger, for better or for worse, will not by itself create social and political attitudes. But a day's or a month's experiences of such signs might. As public citizens we at least need to be vigilant as to the meanings and possible effects of the messages we encounter. Close reading can help us do that. We can thus claim that the ability to read closely is a public, civic responsibility for all of us.

Second, close reading is important *personally.* My ability to get along with my friend may well be improved if I can fully understand the ways his language use differs from mine. Paying attention to differences may alert me to other language variations I encounter, such as the British, in which one lives *"in* Hampton Street," as opposed to the American usage, in which one lives *"on* Hampton Street." We have all probably had other experiences in which the ability to read people and their messages was important. When we were young, we likely needed to pay close attention to our parents and read their tones of voice, words, and actions so that we could learn, grow, and stay out of trouble. Many of us have had difficult bosses or supervisors who needed to be closely read to make the workday go more smoothly. Learning how to read the messages of others more closely is therefore also a valuable personal skill.

Many of the readers of this book are college students. Students have particular need of skills in close reading. If you are a student, seldom in your life will you be in so diverse a group of people, and the ability to read others and their messages is important. Many of you will keep blogs or post messages through such currently popular sites as Facebook or Twitter. The ability to read these very short messages of others may alert you to important dimensions of personality or social beliefs of people you are getting to know or to changes in how old friends think as they go through college. Is a recent blog posting sarcastic? Should you take it seriously? Is the poster angry? Or perhaps seductive? An ability to read closely may help you answer questions like these. And of course, the ability to read a syllabus or course assignment carefully and understand it can make a big difference in your success or failure in college.

Chapters 1 and 2 introduce you to the general subject of close reading. In this first chapter, the section titled "Being a Reader, Being a Critic" explains in more detail what I mean by close reading, and it introduces you to the idea that we read closely in our daily lives. This book will help you to read closely in more disciplined and systematic ways. Further, this chapter discusses what it means to be a critic. It also introduces the idea of rhetoric, or persuasion, and why a better understanding of the rhetoric of what we read is an important goal of close reading.

Chapter 2 explains the concepts of theories, methods, and techniques. For many, these may sound like three difficult concepts, but actually we use them in everyday life. I explain that a *theory* is like a map to a text and that you have likely already learned several theories about how texts work. If you have studied small group communication, for instance, you may have learned theories that help you navigate a group meeting, understanding what is going on as people communicate. A *method* is the vehicle you use to navigate a text, so to speak, following the theory's map. You might use methods of ethnography, for instance, to study a small group as it meets. And *techniques* are habits, tricks, or skills you acquire to study things—for instance, ways of recording conversations in small groups. These key terms are organized conceptually so that you can see how you can use the knowledge you have already gained in your education to support close readings. Additionally, these and other key terms and concepts are italicized in the text and summarized at the end of this chapter.

Chapter 2 also explains the ethical implications of close reading for both critic and audience. Critics and their audiences risk something when they read closely, and they ask others to take similar risks—hence the ethical implications. The chapter discusses both inductive and deductive theories and shows how methods connect to theories.

Finally, the chapter introduces the idea of techniques, which are the focus of the rest of the book.

Chapter 3 explores the idea of form. You will learn that *form* is the structure, the pattern, that organizes a text. Techniques for detecting and understanding form in texts are explained. The three main techniques you will study in Chapter 3 are narrative, genre, and persona. *Narrative* is, as you will learn, the storylike form of a text. Three elements of narrative are found in texts: *coherence and sequence, tension and resolution,* and *alignment and opposition.* A *genre* is a recurring type of text within a context. You will learn that a genre has recurring *situational* and *stylistic* responses to recurring kinds of *contexts.* One can also think of a genre as a recurring type of narrative. Our final technique is the detection of personae, and you will learn that a *persona* is a role, much like a character in a narrative, that someone (such as a reader or critic) plays in connection to a text.

Chapter 4 uses the idea of transformations to organize some techniques for looking beneath the surface of texts, for seeing what might not be apparent at first glance. We will see that *transformations* are ways in which the ordinary, literal meanings of signs and images are turned—reversed, changed, altered—by readers of texts. Some transformations you will study are called *tropes,* and we will examine techniques for identifying the important, common tropes called *metaphor, metonymy, synecdoche,* and *irony.*

Chapter 5 explains techniques of exploring ideology by analyzing the arguments in texts. *Ideology* is a systematic network of beliefs, commitments, values, and assumptions that influence how power is maintained, struggled over, and resisted. Ideologies are supported by and also revealed through argument. *Argument* is a process by which speakers and writers, together with audiences, make claims about what people should do and assemble reasons why people should do those things. You will learn that some good techniques for detecting the arguments that establish ideologies are found in these questions to ask of a text: What should the reader think or do? What must the text ask the reader to assume? How does the reader know what the text claims? Who is empowered or disempowered? With these techniques we may think more critically and productively about the good reasons texts give us for believing what they want us to believe.

Finally, a conclusion brings together many of these techniques to show how they might work together in a close reading. Although it is impossible to use all the techniques in a single close reading, the conclusion illustrates how techniques from across the chapters might be used. The text read will be a cartoon from the strip *Candorville* that appeared shortly before President Obama's inauguration.

Close reading in a disciplined way is a skill that will serve you well for the rest of your life. By no means is it merely an academic exercise. In a world in which messages increasingly ask us to believe, accept, buy, and follow, the ability to read texts closely is an indispensable survival skill. Close reading is both personally and socially empowering. Join me now in learning some techniques of close reading.

❖ BEING A READER, BEING A CRITIC

It won't come as any surprise to you when I point out that you are reading: you are reading this book. Reading is something you do every day, but let's think for a minute about what that involves. You are looking at this book, an object, that is full of black marks on white paper. Not just any black marks; these marks have *meaning*. You know what these black marks mean in the English language, and you know how to put together into a coherent message the meanings that these marks suggest. We can think of *meaning* as the thoughts, feelings, and associations that are suggested by words, images, objects, actions, and messages. Consider this series of ink marks on paper:

DOG

When you read it, certain thoughts, feelings, and associations come into your head, which are what the markings (the letters) mean. That is how all reading works. If you couldn't find meaning in reading (and sometimes we cannot!), you'd quit doing it.

It's a remarkable thing about reading that a hundred people who read the same thing will likely find both the same meanings *and* different meanings. This is true even in ordinary conversation. The last time you said, "I didn't mean that," you were complaining that somebody read a meaning in something you said that you would not find there yourself and that you certainly didn't intend anyone to find. But despite the recurrence of misunderstandings and misreadings, we continue to read books, movies, TV shows, and each other with confidence that we will find enough of the same meanings others would find that we can all make sense of the world together.

Although you know there is a lot of disagreement and "slippage" regarding what messages mean, you are fairly confident that you are finding many of the same meanings in this passage that I, your author, hope you will find there. You are also fairly confident that you are finding many of the same meanings most other people would get from this reading. If somebody else reading this book told you, "You know, the first paragraph is a coded message from that Brummett fellow that the world will end in 2020," you would be justified in doubting such a reading. Although it's not foolproof, we read just exactly to discover meanings that we think most other people would also find if they read the same way we did.

When we read, we do lots of complicated things at once:

- We examine an object (like a book) to figure out some of the things it means.

- We usually (although not always) try to figure out which meanings the person who created that object wanted us to find.

- We usually are interested in finding meanings that other readers who share some of our experiences and contexts would also find.

A *reading*, then, is an attempt to understand the socially shared meanings that are supported by words, images, objects, actions, and messages. Somebody might well think that my first paragraph means that the end of the world is impending, but that is likely not a *socially shared* meaning, since hardly anyone else will find that meaning in the paragraph. A reading is an attempt to find *reasonable* or *plausible* meanings in a message or object, and readings are done in such a way as to be *defensible* after the fact. By *defensible* I mean that someone can produce evidence to support your reading from the message or from widespread usage. You might defend a reading by saying, for instance, "I read the message this way because of the way these two sentences are phrased" or "In the southern United States, most people see that image this way." There is a connection between the fact that we search for socially shared meanings and the fact that we search for meanings that are also plausible and defensible: In everyday reading, we want to read so that most people who encounter the same message could see the same meanings if they, too, were to read the same things. If you get a party invitation that says "semiformal," and you show up in suit and tie while your host greets you at the door in a swimsuit, you will surely defend your reading (that is, give evidence for your understanding) of the invitation as correct, as what most people would find in such a message, and as the meaning most people would intend by "semiformal."

A reader is a *meaning detective,* and while detectives may often make guesses about the mysteries they try to solve, those are usually *educated* guesses that can be backed up with evidence; the same is true for the meaning detective of a message. The meanings we detect are the plausible, defensible, socially shared meanings that are supported by a message. Like detectives, though, we can make educated guesses about meaning, and to do so you must be educated! That is the purpose of this book: to give you some ways to read plausible, socially shared meanings and share them with others in ways you may not now be able to.

It may come as a bit of a surprise when I suggest that you read many other kinds of experiences, some of them clearly messages and some of them not, in ways similar to the way you are reading this book. You see a garden bed all trampled down and read that as meaning that the neighbor's dog has been rolling in it again. You enter your apartment to find pizza boxes here and there and clothes in need of laundering on the floor, and you read that to mean that your roommate has come back early from a visit home. When you go to the movies, think of the screen as an enormous book with each new scene a different page. You see images, you hear dialogue and sounds, and you read them as you would a book. You see a character in a movie pull out a pistol, and you know to read the pistol as meaning the threat of violence. Two characters kiss tenderly, and you read those images as meaning love or affection. As with a book, you are fairly confident that the makers of the film meant you to find these meanings, and you are confident that the people you are with are drawing generally the same meanings from their readings of the movie. If one of your friends shrieked aloud at the sight of a tender kiss and whispered, "Oh! I'm so afraid!" you might wonder at her reading and think that she had found some meanings in the movie unlikely to be shared by other viewers.

In a similar way, you read your boss and coworkers, you read your family members and the gatherings at which you meet them, and you read the music you listen to. You read using techniques of deciphering meaning that are generally, although sometimes not universally, shared among a community of readers: the public, other people who more or less share your experiences, people who have been exposed to the same messages that you have. It would not be too much to claim that any society, any culture, depends on its members sharing roughly similar ways of reading a wide range of experiences. Nor would it be too much to claim that an ability to read is essential to your own happiness and your ability to function socially. Think of what it would be like if you did not know how to decipher the meanings of your friends' gestures and expressions or if you could not share in an understanding of what that new hit comedy on TV last night meant to your coworkers. It would be as if you lived in a country where you spoke none of the language and understood none of the gestures people used. Think how isolated you would be without the ability to read in this broad sense of the term.

Although nearly everybody reads messages and experiences in one way or another, you know from your own experience that there are times when you have to slow down and pay special attention to what you are reading. Did you ever read a book in which there were so many characters in different relationships and with so many different personalities that you had to slow your reading down or read certain passages over again carefully to make sure you understood who was connected to whom and in what way? Many people experience this kind of complexity in the *Harry Potter* series of novels by J. K. Rowling, and they find that slow, careful reading and rereading of the books reveals new understandings. Did you ever see a movie more than once because you felt that there were meanings and dimensions of the film that needed to be understood better—and perhaps you found that paying close attention to a movie the second or third time through helped you to read things you hadn't read before, to see meanings you hadn't seen before? The *Lord of the Rings* and the *Matrix* series of movies affect many people this way, as does the *Lost* television series, and they find that seeing the films or shows over and over again allows them to find new meanings each time.

This second, more careful kind of reading we call a *close reading*. There is no sudden, distinct threshold one crosses to go from a reading to a close reading. The more care and deliberation one takes, the more one studies the words, images, actions, objects, and other components of what one is reading, the more one is closely reading. The move from reading to close reading is a continuum. *Close reading* is mindful, disciplined reading of an object with a view to deeper understanding of its meanings; often, that understanding is shared with others in the form of a *criticism* or *critical analysis*. This book is about the techniques we use when we engage in and share close readings of texts. We are proceeding on the assumption that it is possible to learn techniques of close reading that help you get more out of a message and share what you learn with others in a critical analysis.

What do we want to call the "thing" that you are reading when you read? Of course, we could call it what it is—a movie, a textbook, a country-western tune, and so forth. Let's agree on one overall term for all these things: you are reading a *text*. A *text* is the object that generates the meanings you want to know more about and perhaps tell others about. Knowing how to read carefully and then systematically tell others about a text is what makes a *critic* out of a *reader*. We will explore the concept of being a critic a little later.

There are complications we need to consider when we read a text, however. Two important ones are context and audience. The *context* is what is going on in the surroundings when we read. I mean surroundings in at least two senses here: the *historical* context and the *textual* context. People who read texts are influenced by what is going on historically—not necessarily in the sense of a grand sweep of hundreds of years, but in the sense of what is going on socially, politically, in the day's events. A text that is a movie about a terrorist attack will be read differently the morning after an actual terrorist attack than it will the morning before it. For example, since 9/11, news reports of downed airplanes almost always say whether a terrorist attack is suspected. A haunted house story will be read differently on a bright sunny day than on a stormy night. These are examples of how *historical* contexts affect readings. *Textual* contexts also affect readings. If we are reading a book that has been ironic, playful, and funny all along, we are much more likely to read further passages of the book as ironic, even if they appear to be in deadly earnest. If a vampire appears in a comic movie, we might laugh at it; if a vampire appears in a movie that has been full of werewolves and ghosts, we may cover our eyes in fright. Texts often set up their own contexts that guide readings.

I noted earlier that readers attempt to arrive at plausible, socially shared readings. But it is important to realize that not everyone reads texts in the same way. The reader may need to qualify his or her reading by describing the audience perspective from which a particular interpretation of the text may be derived. A news story about an earthquake in China may be read differently by people of Chinese heritage than by other people. A story about the world's richest human will be read differently according to readers' economic class. Although texts often contain widely shared meanings, honesty and accuracy require the reader to be clear about the audience perspective from which a reading takes place. In other words, the close reader should not assume that his or her reading of a text is necessarily what the text means to others.

Now let's get a little practice in close reading—or, more accurately, let's remind ourselves of what we do when we read closely. Please take a look at the *Baldo* cartoon in Figure 1.2. Think about what happens as you read this text, understand it, and snatch a bit of truth and humor from it. You have to examine all the words and images that make up

Figure 1.2

To view this image in full resolution, please visit www.sagepub.com/brummettstudy.

this text, and for such a small block of space in the daily newspaper, there is actually quite a bit of information that you must process. What is key to making the cartoon work as an insightful and humorous text? Of course, it is the contrast between Baldo's upbeat, inclusive words and the picture of what is in fact a segregated high school cafeteria, with Hispanics, African Americans, and European Americans at separate tables.

Now, think for a moment of some ways to read this cartoon that would miss the "punch line." You could look at it and simply say, "Oh, Baldo is mistaken, the text is showing us how foolish some teenagers can be." Or you could say, "Clearly, the artist in the cartoon wasn't paying attention to the words; this is just a mistake on the part of the makers of the cartoon." But these interpretations are not likely to be most people's. More to the point, these are implausible and not very defensible.

Most people who have spent a significant amount of time in this country will realize the poignant truth in the cartoon: that, although we celebrate diversity in our talk, our personal lives and actual practices often are not so diverse. Awareness of the contradictions that occur in life in a diverse culture is the bundle of meanings we will likely pull out of this reading. We say we appreciate other cultures but then flock together with birds of our own feather when it comes time for lunch, worship, or marriage. I'm guessing that nearly all of us know this to be true with such clarity that we are confident that the cartoonists meant us to recognize that sad discrepancy between what is said and what is done in the cartoon and to recognize that it applies to our lives. I'm guessing that nearly all of us know that others have seen the same cafeterias (or playgrounds or churches) come into conflict with the same hopeful talk. So we are not only confident that the creators of this text intended us to find meanings exposing the contradictions between talk and practice, we are also confident that others in the United States will see the same contradiction and recognize it as a widespread fact of life.

We should also take into consideration the historical and textual contexts within which the cartoon might be read. The course of race relations changes over time, and the presence or absence of some startling news event having to do with race may affect how we read the cartoon. This cartoon appeared before the election of President Obama, for example. How might it be read differently now than when it was first printed? The cartoon occurs within the textual context of the comic strips of a newspaper, which would encourage the reader to approach this text lightheartedly. And, of course, the reader needs to be careful about the audience perspective from which the text is read: How might readers who are members of the different groups portrayed here read the cartoon differently?

But could we go deeper? What would a closer reading look like? We may already be closer in our reading practices than most average viewers of the strip in the morning paper, but let us think about what a close reading entails. Such a reading depends on recognition of some rather detailed and complicated components of the text. For instance, we recognize the different styles that Baldo calls our attention to in the artist's depiction of the three cultural groups. The European American, Hispanic, and African American groups have distinct clothing styles, different postures; if you look closely enough, they even have different facial expressions or gestures by group. Now, are these stereotypes about these ethnic groups, or are they truthful generalizations, perhaps the very reason for the discrepancy between Baldo's words of inclusion and the scene of segregation? Our answer to that question has a lot to do with who the text asks us to be. Are we the kind of people who would sit in separate groups, as do the young people of the cartoon? Or are we called on by the text to be wiser than that and to recognize the need to overcome social habits if we want to live up to Baldo's words? What is there in the text that gives you some clues as to who the text is inviting us to be?

Likewise, is there anything in the text that invites us to stand beside Baldo in his sentiments, or are we meant to take a stance superior to his? Are we called to see ourselves in his words or to take a smug position and recognize how mistaken he is? Who, then, is the text calling us to be in terms of his words as well as the picture?

All that insight from a quick look at a cartoon! That's what we do when we read. And when we read closely, we probe even deeper into texts to extract meanings. We could not yet call our reading of this cartoon a disciplined one, and you may recall from our earlier definition that a close reading is *a mindful, disciplined reading of an object or text*. We will turn in the next chapter to the kinds of tools that can discipline our minds and guide us systematically through close readings. First, let's look at another step we might take in the process of reading: critiquing.

From Reading to Critiquing

Some people keep moving along that continuum of reading into close reading regularly, perhaps habitually. These people are often on the alert for extra dimensions of meaning. They seem to have a knack, or maybe they use rules of thumb or guidelines, for finding meanings that may not be apparent on a first reading but become clearer after a close reading. Such people become interesting to others and of service to others when they share these insights. Let's call these dedicated close readers by the name *critic*. A critic is not critical in the sense of being negative but rather in the sense of critiquing meanings based on a close reading.

Critics come in two forms: professional and everyday. We are used to professional critics, or dedicated close readers. These are the people who offer close readings for us of movies, books, sports, and so forth on blogs, on television, and in newspapers.

Professional critics are all around us, and if you think about it for a moment, you'll realize that you may be more familiar with critics than you think. Do you ever read the opinion page of the local newspaper? Then you will read critiques sent in by local critics in the Letters to the Editor column as well as critiques written by members of the paper's editorial staff. Nationally syndicated columnists often offer critiques as well. For instance, Leonard Pitts is a widely read columnist based in Miami. Take a look at some of his recent columns at http://www .miami.com/mld/miamiherald/living/columnists/leonard_pitts/. Not all these pieces are critiques of a text, but some are. Notice how many of them are based on sharing the results of a close reading of a reader's e-mail, the president's speech, or the commentary of a television pundit. Another place we find critics is on the radio. National Public Radio often airs critiques by Frank Deford and others, which

you may find at http://www.npr.org/templates/archives/archive.php?
thingId=1055&startNum=15. Note how often these critiques are based
on a close reading of the texts of a recent game or a statement or
performance by a sports figure. The Internet Movie Database, at
http://www.imdb.com/, often includes critiques that go beyond mere
reviews, offering brief close readings of current movies in theaters and
DVDs.

You can be an everyday critic, however. An everyday critic is not a
job you apply for. You have likely been a critic yourself, based on a
close reading. Perhaps you know how to read baseball games closely,
and when sitting in the stands, you called a friend's attention to a strategy that was developing on the field. Maybe you follow a soap opera
closely, and while watching one with your sister, you offered her your
take on why that character is being such a jerk. Just as we can all learn
to read closely in our everyday lives, so we can all become critics who
read closely regularly and share our insights with others.

Everyone reads, and everyone has the potential to critique. When
we critique, we figure out a way to share our reading with others. We
become *critics*. We offer other people special insights or knowledge into
some object or experience. All of us read movies, music, television
shows, Internet sites, and books. Not everyone critiques professionally;
not everyone is a paid critic. A critic is someone equipped with special
ways of sharing readings with others, but the critique also involves a
commitment to teach others how to read. A critic is the friend who sits
next to you in a movie theater and points out things about the movie
that you may not have noticed, links actions and characters together in
ways you had not considered, and—unless he or she makes a pest of
herself in doing so—adds to your understanding and enjoyment of that
movie. A critic is not necessarily negative and is not focused on finding
fault. A critic has seen something new and wants others to see it as well.
A *critic* may be defined as a person who is trained in close reading and
in sharing those readings with others. If a reader is a meaning detective,
then a critic is a Sherlock Holmes, an Hercule Poirot, an Adrian Monk
of close reading. And that can be you in your everyday life!

What does a critic do, exactly? If you know a friend is going to a
movie, you might ask which theatre he is going to. "Westgate," he will
reply. Your friend is not yet functioning as a critic. He has given you
some information you had before, but it is information in a form
already understood by all and easily discoverable in that form by going
online or looking in the newspaper. Similarly, if your friend says, "The
first show is at 7," that is not a critique but rather a factual—and useful—
statement. Neither statement required close readings of anything.

Figure 1.3

To view this image in full resolution, please visit www.sagepub.com/brummettstudy.

Your friend becomes a critic when he comes back from the movie, and you ask him how it was. Let's suppose he replies, "You know it was one of those *Star Tussle* movies set in outer space, but it occurred to me that it was really a Western in disguise. The spaceship was like a covered wagon going through dangerous territory toward a distant, promised land. They had to repel all sorts of threats from other beings and from natural forces. They all carried weapons, which were used a lot. Yup, just like a Western." Now, your friend has become a critic. Why? Your friend is sharing with you *a way to see a text* that you did not have before. Your friend knows *a way to read texts* that enables him to give you *knowledge* about the text that you did not have before.

The *Mother Goose and Grimm* cartoon in Figure 1.3 is an example of a widespread attitude toward messages, especially such entertaining texts as *Tom and Jerry* cartoons. The idea that there are "no hidden messages" in a text just because it is a cartoon or a television show or even a commercial is mistaken, if common. In fact, we might closely read this very cartoon for a such meanings. Note the old-fashioned television set, a big boxy type that is no longer made. Note the large pattern on the overstuffed chair, which looks dated and homey. Note that the chair is pulled right up to the television set. We see no other furniture, no sofa on which a number of people might sit. The cartoon conveys meanings of a single, perhaps even lonely, older person who is not concerned about having up-to-date technology or stylish furniture in the home. One might wonder if that is the kind of audience the cartoon wants to attract: an older, more conservative demographic. So there we are: Although the cartoon characters may find no hidden meanings in *Tom and Jerry,* there may be hidden meanings in their own little world! It is legitimate for critical close readers to search for such meanings anywhere.

A little earlier we defined a critic as one who is trained in close reading and in sharing those readings with others. What is the critic trained to do, or how is a critic trained in seeing a text differently from others? This way to see a text, this "thing" that can generate knowledge, we will call a *technique of criticism*. Anyone can learn these techniques, as you will in this book. We begin talking about techniques and how to use them in close reading in a later chapter. It is methods and related concepts that give us the discipline that moves us from reading to close reading.

Communication of insights about the meaning of a text is therefore an important dimension of being a critic. Why do we share these insights? Critics want to share their insights about the meanings of texts because they have understood that they live more richly, with more awareness, when they arrive at these insights, and they want others to have the same advantages. Critics therefore serve an important public function—whether the public is the nation or just a group of friends watching a makeover show—of opening people's eyes to hidden depths and dimensions of meaning. You can serve that function yourself in everyday life.

Let's get some quick practice in being a critic; later in this book we will learn in more detail the discipline of methods and techniques that can make us critics. But for the moment, try this exercise: think about a text you have experienced (TV show, movie, song, Internet site) that was a fairy tale in disguise. Of course, you'll have to think about what makes something a fairy tale, even if it is in disguise—that is, even if it's not really about witches and elves and fairies and dark forests and so forth, it's still a fairy tale. No fair saying that you watched a DVD of "Little Red Riding Hood" on that last visit to your little cousins—we already know that's a fairy tale; you don't need to do a close reading to realize that. Let me give you a hint. How do some of the *Star Wars* movies (especially the first one) begin? Why, with these words: "A long time ago in a galaxy far, far away." Now, what does that sound like? Does the parallel to fairy tales continue throughout that and other movies? No fair using this example; you got it for free, so find another one: What's some other text you have seen recently that is a fairy tale in disguise, and why is it one?

Now, let's think about what good it does to say that such and such a text is a fairy tale in disguise. When you have shared that insight with others, even when you have arrived at the insight yourself, what have you and others learned? How are your lives enriched? Think about these things:

- New meanings you can see in the text that you couldn't see before, enabled by that statement. If you start to develop the idea of what it means to be a fairy tale, do even more new meanings begin to surface out of the text?

- The possible fruitfulness of asking the fairy-tale question about other texts.

- The possible fruitfulness of asking similar questions about other texts (What texts are commentaries on interracial relationships in disguise? What texts are like boxing matches in disguise?).

- The possibility of new ways to think or act, even small ones, that you or your friends might gain from the insights you have had. What difference in your lives might those insights create?

The more enthusiastically and thoroughly you have acted like a critic, the more you will see how your thinking about these issues reveals insights and has the potential to make a difference. That such benefits might befall other people, too, is the reason why people would want to engage in critique and communicate their insights to others.

The question might reasonably arise, Why do we need close readers and critics to discover socially shared meanings? In other words, if the meanings are socially shared, won't people already know about them? What, really, does a critical close reader do that the average person on the street does not do? I argue that the close-reading critic reveals *meanings that are shared but not universally* and also *meanings that are known but not articulated.* The benefit of revealing such meanings is to *teach* or *enlighten* those who hear or read the critique.

First, just because social meanings are shared does not mean they are universally shared. A critical close reader is able to expand people's knowledge of socially shared meanings by calling their attention to meanings that not everyone shares. A former student and friend of mine who is gay once told me that the *X-Men* series of movies is actually about the theme of "coming out," or revealing one's sexuality to a sometimes hostile world. This friend told me he thought that most gay and lesbian people would find such meanings there. He explained that many of the themes of the films have to do with choices to reveal or not to reveal one's difference and with how to handle the consequences of others' knowing that you have "special powers." I had no idea! Since he called my attention to those meanings, seeing the *X-Men* films again has confirmed his close reading for me. I now see meanings that I would not have seen before. The more this student shares his critical close readings with others, the more widely the net expands of people who will know to find those meanings in those films.

A critical close reader is also able to call to people's attentions meanings that they know but have not articulated. Sometimes we "know" those meanings at a level that is nearly subconscious, but the critical close reader can help us recover what we, at some level, already know. All of us have had the experience of having a vague hunch about a text, a public figure or event, a feeling that something is going on beyond what meets the eye, but we haven't quite been able to put it into words. Think of the movie you want to watch again and again but could not explain why. Think of the political leader you mistrust but cannot say why. Think of the television evangelist you trust but cannot say why. Critical close readers are good at helping people clarify the socially shared meanings generated by these texts.

Both of these ways in which the close-reading critic reveals socially shared meanings to us are *epistemological*: they are ways of arriving at knowledge. The epistemology (or logic of knowing) that critical close reading depends on is based on *teaching* and *plausibility*. The critical close reader is a teacher of those who read or hear the critique. The critic's job is to uncover these meanings in such a way that people have an "aha!" moment in which they suddenly agree to the reading, the meanings the critic suggests suddenly come into focus. The meanings seem plausible to the hearer or reader. The standard of success for the close reader who is also a critic is therefore the *enlightenment, insights,* and *agreement* of those who hear or read what he or she has to say.

The Calling to Be a Critic

Some people have what you might say is a kind of *calling* or *vocation* to be a critic. People refer to a calling or a vocation in describing the feeling of commitment held by those who enter religious orders, who devote their lives to spiritual work and service. But those terms have application beyond religious contexts. You might say that someone really has a calling to be a baker. Or someone might tell you that he or she works in a grocery store but that his or her vocation is to be a poet. An important dimension of a calling is that it never leaves you; if you have a calling to be an architect, then you are nearly always thinking about structures, shapes, and designs. You move through the world studying buildings, if your vocation is to be an architect. If your job is to be a small-engine mechanic, you might stop being a mechanic at 5:00 p.m. and become something else. But if your calling or vocation is to be a small-engine mechanic, you go home to study journals and magazines on engine repair, you go online to find chat rooms or Usenet groups of other mechanics, and you take an interest in your neighbor's balky lawnmower.

Being a critic can be a kind of calling. Most committed critics are not professional; they are just committed to close reading, to paying attention. The really good critics are always on the lookout for messages and experiences that repay a close reading. Not all experiences do, of course; you get tired pretty quickly of giving careful attention to the back of a soup can. But many of life's everyday messages and experiences do repay a close reading. A true critic in this sense is often "on," always thinking about ways in which the extra attention of close reading might reveal meanings and dimensions of books, movies, television shows, and so forth.

The critic is often "on" because of a conviction that the meanings of messages and experiences are important. The critic assumes that this music video, this movie, this wedding ceremony is influencing or affecting people and that the meanings one can find in those experiences are key to that influence. The critic wants to know about these often complex dimensions of meanings because understanding them is a way to understand how our attitudes, actions, perceptions, and predispositions are formed. The critic is on a mission to inform self and others about what messages and experiences are "doing" to us so as to shape how we think and act.

An important part of a critic's calling is the openness to consider a wide range of texts and the commitment to devote the attention and energy of close reading to texts that will repay the effort. We should be open to the possibility that the label on a soup can, to use an earlier example, might repay a close reading—that we might find some interesting meanings and important possible influences on that soup can. But if an attempt at close reading fails to show such wonders on the soup can label, the critic will also give it up, reserving the effort for texts that are rich enough or deep enough to repay a critic's attention.

The concern with how people are influenced is sometimes summed up under the term *rhetoric*. *Rhetoric* is an ancient term denoting the study of ways in which people are persuaded or influenced. Throughout history, people have been influenced in different ways, from public speaking to advertisements to political debates, and the study of rhetoric has included all of these communicative experiences. One can be a critic and want to know about many different dimensions of messages and experiences: aesthetic dimensions, psychological dimensions, and so forth. But if you want to know more about what messages and experiences mean because you are interested in how people's thoughts and actions are influenced, how people are persuaded, then you are a *rhetorical critic*. The calling of the rhetorical critic, then, becomes a mission to say to self and others, "Look! This movie, this song on this disc, supports these meanings that you may not have thought of before. . . ."

For instance, I just took a break from writing after that last paragraph and walked through my living room, where my daughter had the television on. A commercial for bottled water was proclaiming, "The best things in life are pure." Hmmm. . . . now, the casual reader of that advertisement might shrug and say, "Yes, I guess so, whatever." Which, of course, is what the sellers of the water want people to do. I stopped and spent some time reading that simple phrase in my head closely. I think there are some meanings in there that we need to be aware of and think about, and they cause me to wonder, What does *pure* mean? Does it mean "composed of all one thing"? If something different enters into the nature of a thing, does that make it impure? What does this mean in regard to people of more than one racial background? Does it make them "impure"? What does this mean in regard to complicated questions, such as whether or in what way to go to war? If someone thinks the matter is not simple but has many contradictory issues wrapped up together, is that "impure" thinking? Suppose we have a population that is trained by television commercials like that one to think that *pure* equals *simple* and thus that *simple* equals *good*. Would that population think of the world in black-and-white terms, with no shades of gray? And so on and so forth. As a critic, I often think about what experiences and messages mean because I think that their meanings affect people in powerful ways. And if I get the chance, I'll share these insights with others because I want them to see the texts in their lives more richly. In fact, I just did that with you!

Another example: I was online and found a link to a movie review. The title suggested that the reviewer "tries to find deeper meaning in the new *Lara Croft* movie." That reviewer must be a critic: someone interested in telling the public about movies and what they mean. Of course, the public itself is fully capable of going to movies and reading them, but someone who is offering up "deeper meanings" is going to do a closer reading of a movie than is the guy sitting there with his feet up enjoying the popcorn. The reviewer is a professional critic and gets paid for close readings. Most critics do not get paid money for close readings. As a calling, it becomes woven into one's way of life to probe into messages and share those deeper meanings with others. That is the kind of habit this book wants to encourage you to take up: to be always ready for a close reading, to become a critic. If one is not paid a salary for doing it, then one is paid in enlightenment, in the ability to see deeper levels of meaning and to share those insights with others.

To be a rhetorical critic gives us another level of understanding of the concept of meaning. Earlier we defined *meaning* as the thoughts, feelings, and associations that are suggested by words, images, objects, actions, and messages. If your interests are rhetorical, then you also think of meaning as what words, images, objects, actions, and messages do to people's thoughts, motives, attitudes, and predispositions. If I refer to a certain political candidate as a dog, then the meanings of *dog* that I am attaching to that candidate will be what my statement does to you. To think rhetorically is to think of meaning as powerful, as affecting people. Of course, that is another important reason to be a critic for yourself and others, so you can help people understand what texts are doing to them.

From Critiquing to Communicating

I have said several times that communicating the results of a close reading to other people is what turns a reader into a critic. In this section I invite you to think creatively, with a sense of possibilities, about ways that you can function as a critic and thus communicate your insights to others. You may have a sense that there are, indeed, critics in this world but only an elite few who write for magazines and newspapers or appear on television—such people as professional movie or restaurant reviewers, political or opinion columnists, and the like. You may have a sense that there are few outlets for your own critical voice to be heard. Nothing could be farther from the truth. Even before we begin to learn specific techniques of close reading, you need to understand that your voice can be heard in a variety of ways. Let's organize our survey of "ways to be heard" according to the media in which you might express yourself: *You can be a critic on the Internet, in print, and in person.*

Critiquing on the Internet   Going online is a wonderful way to share your critiques with others. Potentially thousands, if not millions, of people might be informed by your insights on a global scale. There are at least three ways you can use this powerful medium to share your critiques with the world.

First, you can create your own Web site. This is not necessarily free, especially if you want a high-quality site, and it may require a certain amount of technical skill. So creating a Web site might be a less attractive option for some. But it is still a definite possibility for many people.

On a Web site you can put commentaries and illustrate them with visual images, links to other Web sites that might allow downloads of television or movie material, and so forth. This lets you couple your critique with samples of the text that you might be critiquing, which may have more impact on your audience than a critique alone.

How to set up a Web site is well beyond the scope of this book, but there are a number of resources online for finding out how to do it. You can go to a search engine such as www.google.com and simply type in "create a Web site," and all sorts of currently available services will pop up for you to explore. Typing in that request at this writing generated many such services, of which these are but a few:

http://www.make-a-web-site.com/

http://www.2createawebsite.com/

http://www.ipage.com/

http://www.homestead.com/?s_cid=G130023B

Sites such as Facebook allow fairly easy creation of a presence online. Go check it out!

Second, you can start a blog, short for Weblog, which is actually a very specific kind of Web site on which people can record their daily thoughts and reactions, post photos, and so forth. Many people treat their blogs as a sort of online diaries. Blogs are widely read and have been invaluable sources of information for many people, as bloggers around the world keep the public informed about political and social developments and even natural disasters and upheavals. If there is a revolution, hurricane, or tsunami in some part of the world, people often seek out bloggers to find out what is going on from the perspective of the "person on the street." For this reason, critics who share their views on blogs can find a ready audience. Once again, typing in "create a blog" on a search engine such as Google will yield a number of current services. At this writing, such a search found these sites, among many others:

http://www.createblog.com/

http://rsstoblog.com/

http://www.blogger.com/start

http://www.sixapart.com/typepad/start

Third, you can join a Usenet group, bulletin board, or discussion room and participate in ongoing discussions in which you can share your critiques. This is an especially useful tool for sharing quick, short insights (long posts don't work as well in this format). There are literally thousands of groups and Web sites that allow people to exchange messages on any subject, from politics to poodles to polo horses. Some groups are moderated, with an individual or small group of people responsible for screening possible messages, while others are not. The moderated groups tend to be more useful, as they do not collect huge piles of spam that can get in the way of real discussions. Many Web sites host their own bulletin boards or discussion groups, which also function as small "public places" for discussion. One place to begin locating a group that would suit your interests is Google groups, which at this writing may be found at http://groups.google.com/grphp?hl=en&tab=wg&q=. You can also look for chat room or bulletin board options on some of your favorite Web sites, on any topic. All of these options for discussion groups, bulletin boards, chat rooms, and so forth are excellent places to share short, focused critiques.

Critiquing in Print   Many people may feel that they are shut out of sharing critiques with others in print. We read magazines and see nationally syndicated columns in newspapers, and some people may conclude that they can never participate in a discussion at that level. Although it is true that few can become syndicated columnists who publish critiques on politics, entertainment, or sports in newspapers and magazines on a regular basis, those same printed media are very often open to the general public.

Take newspapers, for instance. Most papers accept letters to the editor or even lengthier opinion pieces written by members of the general public and publish some every day. These venues run the full gamut, from local papers in small communities that may publish only once a week to such papers as the *New York Times* or the *Houston Chronicle*, which may have regional or national distribution. The likelihood of your critique being published in some kind of newspaper is much greater than you might think. Newspapers have the advantage of being timely; in fact, your critique should probably have something to do with current or cultural events that are happening in the moment. Even a week late can mean that the newspaper regards your critique as old news. Examine the newspapers that originate near you to see what these opportunities might be. Look at the editorial pages for letters and longer opinion pieces on topics of current interest. Look in the arts and entertainment pages for reviews written by readers on books, films, television shows, restaurants, and so forth. Many newspapers even publish letters on sports-related subjects in the sports pages. Pay close attention to the styles and topics that are preferred by these newspapers, as these may vary considerably from paper to paper.

Magazines are harder to be published in, but some may regard a critique published in a magazine as of higher status. Magazines often pay their contributors; you could be well on your way to fame and fortune as a regular writer! It is especially important to examine the magazine to which you intend to submit your work, to get a sense of the style and topics the magazine prefers. Magazines tend to be more specialized than newspapers, so your critique will need to be a close match to the interests of the publication to which you will submit your work. There are several ways to start. You can't do better than to go to a local newsstand—or even a magazine rack in a nearby library, grocery, or drugstore—to examine the array of likely magazines. You can also go online to the *Writer's Digest* Web site (at http://www.writersdigest.com/) or find a hard copy in a bookstore. *Writer's Digest* is a useful guide to a wide range of magazines, and it also contains helpful advice on how to write and publish in magazines.

You can get good information on how to publish in magazines and other venues, as well as good feedback from others interested in critiques, by looking for local or regional writer's associations. These groups often host workshops on how to publish. They often hold short courses on writing that can strengthen your critiquing skills. Just a few examples include writer's associations in Southern California (http://www.ocwriter.com/), Texas (http://www.writersleague.org/), Florida (http://www.floridawriters.net/), and New York (http://www.nywriterscoalition.org/).

Think also about newsletters or bulletins that may be locally produced for very small audiences. A school or neighborhood association newspaper, the bulletin or newsletter for a church, synagogue, or mosque or the local publication of a social or civic club might be an outlet for critiques of a very focused sort. It helps if you are a member of the organization putting out the publication.

Many of you may be reading this book in connection with a class, and sharing a critique with your instructor in writing may be a class assignment. Think of this as a good opportunity to influence the instructor, at least. It is also a good practice session for developing a critique that you might share with a wider audience. Reading your critique to others may even be part of a class exercise. You may well have the chance to influence several others just in class through your writing.

Critiquing in Person   The best place for you to practice being a critic may be in person, in your everyday life interactions with friends, family, and coworkers. This is especially true if you develop the calling to be a critic; you will always be thinking about what messages mean, and you will instinctively be doing close readings of texts. You can offer critiques based on those close readings to people you are with while watching television or movies. You can critique important memos or e-mails at work. You can help your relatives understand what another relative is saying by "unpacking" his or her spoken and nonverbal texts. Of course, you want to observe the rules of proper behavior and good taste in all this—few people like someone who is critiquing every minute of the day—but if done in the context of sharing insights with others, a critique based on the habit of close reading can become a way of being for you.

❖ SUMMARY AND LOOKING AHEAD

In this chapter you have learned a number of concepts and definitions. To review, they are as follows:

- *Meaning* is the thoughts, feelings, and associations that are suggested by words, images, objects, actions, and messages.

- A *reading* is an attempt to understand the socially shared meanings that are supported by words, images, objects, actions, and messages.

- In a reading, we identify meanings that are *socially shared, plausible,* and *defensible.*

- A reader is a *meaning detective.*

- *Close reading* is the mindful, disciplined reading of an object with a view to deeper understanding of its meanings.

- Close readings are often shared with others in a *criticism* or *critique.*

- A *text* is the object that generates the meanings you want to know more about and perhaps tell others about.

- Close readings must take into account *context*, both *historical* and *textual.*

- Close readings must take into account the *audience perspective* from which reading occurs.

- A critic may be defined as a person who is trained in close reading and in sharing those readings with others.

- An important part of being a critic is communication of insights about the meaning of a text.
- A critic teaches or enlightens those who hear or read the critique by revealing meanings that are not universally shared and meanings that are known but not articulated.
- It can be a kind of calling or vocation to be a critic.
- Rhetoric is an ancient term denoting the study of ways in which people are persuaded or influenced.
- Opportunities for critiquing are available to you on the Internet, in print, and in person.

You may recall that I briefly mentioned *techniques* earlier, but these concepts are not listed in our summary. That is because I will be developing them, along with the concepts of *method* and *theory*, in the next chapter. Although these ideas may sound rather academic and therefore dull, nothing could be farther from the truth. You will learn in the next chapter how much of what you already know or are learning in other classes can be put to use in close readings.

2

Theories, Methods, Techniques

❖ ❖ ❖

Many people will begin reading a chapter titled "Theories, Methods, Techniques" with a lot of fear and trembling. These sound like difficult and boring topics. The term *theories* seems especially forbidding. Many people are accustomed to thinking of theory as something opposed to practice. In fact, you may think of theory as something completely abstracted from the real world. You might imagine a moldy professor in a tweed jacket muttering to himself in a dark study as he spins theories that are disconnected from the streets outside. To tell the truth, the way some academics write theory lends credence to this fear.

But for most theories, nothing could be further from the truth. *Theories, methods,* and *techniques are ways to figure out the real world.* The best theories, methods, and techniques link together special knowledge about experience and experience itself. At their best, theories, methods, and techniques help us get through the day.

Why are we talking about theories, methods, and techniques in a book on close reading? Because close reading is an exercise in linking special knowledge to experience, and theories, methods, and techniques are kinds of special knowledge. They are knowledge of how to be a meaning detective, how to notice meanings that others might not.

You may recall that we learned this definition in the first chapter: *Close reading is mindful, disciplined reading of an object with a view to deeper understanding of its meanings.* What we will learn in this chapter has to do with that word *disciplined.* Theories, methods, and techniques give the close-reading critic a structure, a *discipline,* in reading that allows meanings to be detected more powerfully and more efficiently. Alternatively, theories, methods, and techniques are sometimes the result of a close reading that enables others to do a disciplined reading (more on this distinction shortly). I want to stress that close reading is possible *without* explicit theories and methods (I believe you always need techniques; more on this, too, shortly). Some people can do a close reading naturally, intuitively. But if you are not used to close reading and find yourself wanting more guidance, this chapter will help you. This chapter explains the relationship of techniques to theories and methods of exploring texts. The chapter helps us understand what a technique is.

❖ EXPLORING NEW TERRITORIES:
    THINKING DEDUCTIVELY AND INDUCTIVELY

By way of a preview of our three key terms—*theory, method,* and *technique*—we might use a travel metaphor. Suppose you are going to explore a part of the country you have not previously visited. Let's say you are going to a distant state, and your goal is to see the sights, to discover what is there. That distant state is like a text you encounter, a text you want to read closely and critically. What "sights" will you find in the text, what interesting meanings that may not be fully apparent? What ways are most useful to you in making your way around either the new state or the text?

Of course, some people will just set out for this new territory extemporaneously. They may have a knack for travel, a good sense of direction. And some people confronted with a text will charge right into it, exercising a natural talent for close reading. But not everyone will enter a new territory or a new text in this way. A lot of people need extra guidance; they need some kind of discipline to help them along.

Many people who are going to a new territory will take a map. *Think of a theory as a map to a text.* There are many different kinds of maps you can take to explore a new territory: road maps, topographical maps, maps of waterways, maps of hiking trails, and so forth. There are also many different theories out there about how texts work and what there is to see. A theory sets the parameters, or the basic assumptions, for how you will move about in the text, so to speak. If you have a map of waterways, then you will go about on rivers and lakes. If you have a road map, you will travel on streets and highways instead. One theory about how a text works might suggest that you pay attention to psychological appeals, while another theory might stress the importance of looking at argument. You can't read everything in texts closely, just as you can't go everywhere and see everything in a new territory, so a map or a theory helps you to set limits for your travel.

So you have a general plan for entering the territory and moving around in it—but how will you move around? You need a *way* to travel. Most people will need some kind of a vehicle for taking advantage of the map, for following the map's instructions. If you have a road map, you still need to figure out what sort of vehicle will most usefully get you around on the roads: a sports car, a four-wheel-drive SUV, a tractor-trailer, a motorcycle. Which vehicle you choose has a lot to do with what the map (theory) says you will encounter and what you want to get out of your trip. *Think of a method as the vehicle you use to get around a text.* If your map tells you there are mud roads where you are going, a Hayabusa "crotch rocket" motorcycle may not be the best bet for transportation. Often, theories call for certain kinds of methods. We'll talk about some examples later in the chapter.

So you have a general plan and overview given to you by your map—or your theory—and you have a vehicle to get around the territory described by your map; call this your method. How will you drive that particular vehicle? What are some tricks to using it most effectively? What does the experienced driver of a given vehicle know that a novice does not? People who drive pick up skills in braking on slippery roads, getting out of mud, parallel parking, and so forth. These are techniques. *Think of techniques of close reading as habits, tricks, and knacks you use "on the ground" once inside a text.* Techniques for driving one vehicle do not always apply to another vehicle (for instance, you stop and turn differently on a motorcycle and in a car). There are also techniques for using methods in critical close reading. These are specific ways of seeing texts that you can develop with study and practice.

Now, it may already have occurred to some of you to object that this business of consulting maps and picking vehicles and learning how to use them is not the only way to explore a territory. You are absolutely right. We have been describing what some would call a *deductive approach.* A deductive approach reasons from general principles to particular cases. We would call this "start with the map" or "start with the theory" method *deductive* because it begins with general principles of theory and works from there to particular texts.

But a top-down, theory-driven approach is not the only way to do a close reading, just as simply charging joyfully into a new territory without a map is not the only way to travel—although somebody had to do just that to be able to draw the map in the first place. Let's look at an alternative to a theory-first, deductive model.

If you approach a text without the initial guidance of a theory and its methods, you may well be working from the "bottom up," examining a specific text to see what can be learned that will be useful to you and others beyond this textual experience. We could call this an *inductive approach*. A critical close reading rarely stops at the text, especially if it finds something interesting to say about the text. The close reading goes beyond the text in criticism, as the critic shares insights. As the critic tells others what he or she has found in the text, the critic may offer others methods for seeing the same thing. If the critic is really onto something, a theory may eventually be formed that provides people with a map to the territory of that text. In the same way, those who drew maps for the first time worked inductively, going from their actual lived experience with a text to eventually constructing maps.

Now, here's a key point: Notice that *techniques* are fundamental to both deductive and inductive approaches. If you work deductively, theory suggests methods, which suggest techniques. If you work inductively, techniques can grow into methods and then into theories. To compare this to the map metaphor, nobody simply goes charging about a new territory with no sense of how to walk, row, or drive. At least you will see that the ground in front of you is rough, and you will put on boots, not flip-flops! You need to have techniques that tell you how to connect to the actual stuff of a territory, and the same is true of close reading. So we need techniques no matter which approach we use. That's why this book is called *Techniques of Close Reading*. We will focus on techniques that are most likely to be shared across different approaches, whether deductive or inductive. With this general overview of how theories, methods, and techniques work, let us look at each term more carefully. We begin as if we were thinking deductively and then talk about the inductive approach later.

❖ STARTING FROM THE TOP, DEDUCTIVELY:
THEORIES AND THEIR METHODS

There are quite a few theories about how texts work to create meanings and influence people. There are old and new theories, academic and popular theories, theories from many fields of study. Psychologist Robert

Cialdini has developed a social scientific theory, based on "judgmental heuristics," that explains how persuasion works in contexts of everyday interaction. Many people in business and sales make use of his theory in applied ways. The ancient scholar Aristotle likewise developed a theory of how to observe in any particular case the available means of persuasion, with a focus on public speaking, and his book on rhetoric is still influential today. In the discipline of English, Wayne C. Booth wrote an important theoretical book on the rhetoric of irony, explaining how irony works in texts ranging from literature to everyday conversation. Another scholar of English, James L. Kinneavy, is known for an important theory of how discourse works. The multidisciplinary scholar Kenneth Burke developed a number of theories of how texts ground our motives and perceptions.

This selection of theories is but a drop in the bucket of the thousands that are available to you. You might think about the range of classes you have taken and the theories that were presented in them. Perhaps you took a course in psychology or film studies and read some of the psychoanalytic theories of Jacques Lacan, which many scholars have found useful in close readings of a wide range of texts, from everyday conversations to film. Perhaps you took a course in sociology and read some of the theories of symbolic interaction developed by Erving Goffman. Useful theories potentially can come from any source in any discipline: biology, economics, art history, comparative literature, and beyond.

Not every theory will be interesting or useful to you, just as not every map will lay out a way to explore a territory that will make for a pleasant trip. Kenneth Burke's theories, for example, generally take the stance that human motives and actions stem from discourse, from the language and nonverbal symbols we use. First comes the way of speaking, then comes our motivation for speaking. Now, not everyone finds that Burke's basic stance makes sense. Some people think that motives and perceptions come first, and we find a discourse to name those motives. That's all right; some theories take that position also. The point is that if you are entering a territory and you are interested in hiking trails, a map of the interstate highway system there will not be of interest to you. There's no sense in getting a map of city streets if the part of the territory you want to enter is the waterways. The same is true of theories that tell us how texts work. They all carry certain assumptions and restrictions, and not every theory will be compatible with how we think about the world or even about the specific texts we want to read. Let's engage in an extended exercise to help you remember the theories to which you have already been exposed and to think about how they might help in close reading.

EXERCISE 2.1

❖ Bring to class an example of a text that you find intriguing, something you think would repay a close reading because you think there are more meanings to it than meet the eye. Bring the means to share the text with others by handing out copies, calling it up online, playing it on a disk, and so forth.

❖ In whatever department you are taking this class (English, Communication Studies, and so on), you are likely to have taken other courses, as are several of your fellow classmates. Brainstorm in groups about some theories of texts, discourse, communication, and interaction that you have studied in other classes in that same department. Come to some agreement that Theory X taught by Professor Pumpernickel out of Professor Ryebread's book in that course last semester seems like a useful way to generalize about how texts work. Feel free to identify more than one theory.

❖ Now, share the examples of texts within the group. Talk about ways in which the theory or theories you have recalled from other courses in that department seem like they might help you explain meanings in a close reading of the texts that people have brought to class. Help each other see the potential for using theory to guide a close reading.

❖ Next, go beyond the department you are in. What are some theories that the people in your group have studied in other departments and other disciplines? Do some of them seem to have some connection with the texts you have brought to class? Could some of them help you do a close reading?

❖ Have fun with a quick close reading of the texts everyone has brought; use a wide variety of theories. Notice how some theories are better maps to some texts than others are. Think about whether the application of a theory to a text in a close reading has helped you to see meanings and influences in the text that you would not otherwise have seen.

A theory is usually not something that can be summed up neatly in a paragraph. It may take a whole article, a book, or even several books to lay out all the details of a theory. How do you know when you have hold of a theory? Here are some key characteristics of theories to look for:

• A theory is a *generalization* that goes beyond particular examples or individual cases. There can be theories about anything: how to get your old car to start, how to succeed in physics courses, how best to sand hardwood boards, how to ask people out successfully, and so forth. Most of the theories used in close reading are theories that make generalizations about how people think or behave. This is especially true for rhetorical close readings, since they look for ways texts influence people's thinking and behavior.

- In generalizing, a theory offers a *coherent rationale* for why things happen as they do or why things are as they are. Whatever a theory says must hold together around a clear, consistent explanation of the world. This is *not* a theory: "My tractor battery died because I haven't run it in a while, and birds make nests under that corner of my roof because nobody ever walks there." To be sure, that nonsensical statement contains generalizations, arguably two of them, but the generalizations have nothing to do with each other or with a generalizable statement of how the world is. There is no coherent rationale about how life works in that statement. Great theories are *powerful* insofar as they give us far-reaching wisdom about life.

- In generalizing, a theory should seem *broadly applicable and useful.* Good theories give us that "Aha!" moment in which we say to ourselves (or others, if we're a critic), "So that's why Aunt Mabel does things the way she does," or "Well, that would account for that last election, wouldn't it?" If you can't tell, with a little work and thought, what it is in life and experience that a theory explains, then you should put that theory down and go find another one.

- A theory can be *disproved.* It can be *disagreed with* by reasonable people. To generalize by saying that the sun may be seen in the east every morning is not a theory, since it is unlikely ever to be shown to be false, and hardly anyone will disagree with that statement. Principles of religious belief are likewise not theories, since they are held on faith—and matters of faith, although they are surely disagreed with by others, are not subject to disproof. To say that a theory can be disproved means that it must be *testable,* it must be connectable with real experience. There can be no meaningful theories about what they have for lunch on the planet Foosbane if one can never go to the planet Foosbane to examine whether the theory is true or not.

- A theory can also be *supported,* and that is precisely what you do in close reading when you use a theory to help you get through the text. You are showing yourself and others the usefulness of that theory in revealing the meanings and influences of a text. Now, not every theory will be supported by every reading. If you find that a particular theory does not help you read a text closely, that does not mean the theory is useless. Similarly, if you find that a hammer won't help you turn a screw, that doesn't mean the hammer is no good—it was just meant for a different job. Only if the hammer never seems useful or applicable, if it is completely "disproved" in some way (it is designed to drive nails, but it never succeeds at that), would you discard the hammer. A reader should take away from your critical close reading a sense that that theory (and methods and techniques) could be used to find meanings in some texts the reader has personally encountered.

In sum, how do you know when you've found a theory? We recognize a theory first by the *generalizations* it makes about the world. We recognize a theory that can help us in close reading usually by the generalizations it makes about how texts create meaning and influence people, or about how the human mind works as it processes texts like those we want to read closely. A useful theory says, "The world of texts works this way and that." If you apply whatever that generalization about texts may be to an actual text, you will find that the theory suggests paths to take in closely reading that text. Again, think of a theory as a map into the text. So the question you should ask is, Does this particular theory give me some instructions that can help me find my way around this particular text? Then ask whether it offers a *coherent rationale* for understanding a wide variety of texts; in other words, is it *broadly applicable and useful*? Finally, we ask whether the theory can be both *disproved* and *supported*; that is, can evidence be cited from actual texts to show that the theory does or doesn't work?

❖ KNOWLEDGE, RISK, AND ETHICS IN THEORIES AND METHODS

When a critic uses a theory to ask you to see something in a text that you did not see before, that person is doing something rather peculiar and marvelous, if you think about it. The critic is telling you that if you will try to understand that thing over there, that text, in terms of this thing over here, this theory, then you will have new knowledge about the text. The theory really is, in this case, a set of words, a language, a vocabulary that you might not have known before. So the critic does asks you to organize the text according to a way of speaking (the theory) that you did not previously know and asserts that this new way of speaking will give you knowledge of the text.

All knowledge works in this way. *All knowledge is translation.* Every class you take gives you a new way of speaking, a new set of terms (this is why you are asked to memorize all those tedious definitions!) so that you can apply those terms to some part of experience, translating the experience into the new set of terms. If you take a class in sociology, the critic—your instructor—will tell you that a certain theory, perhaps Erving Goffman's theory of stigma, will help you to understand what happens when you pass a homeless person on the sidewalk who asks you for money. The experience of passing the homeless person is nothing new to you; it might happen two or three times a day. But the sociology professor is telling you that the ability to speak about that experience in the terms given to us by Goffman *counts as new knowledge about the encounter.* Even science and mathematics courses teach you how to see physical phenomena in terms of numbers and equations. All knowledge is translation.

A method is not only a way for the critic to look for what a theory calls our attention to in a text. Both a theory and a method are also an invitation to the reader or audience of the criticism to think in the same way as the critic. A theory and its method is a structure of thinking, of perception, shared by both critic and reader as they approach a text. *Critic and reader dance together on the floor of the text to the music of the theory and its methods.* This means that the reader needs to be in some measure of sympathy with the critic's theory and method or at least willing to suspend judgment and disbelief long enough to see what sort of dance the critic will lead. I once gave a lecture in which I argued that a certain movie that seems to have nothing to do with race was in fact about racial issues at a formal level. The movie, I argued, was following the form of a widespread liberal myth of racial history in the United States (Brummett, *Rhetorical Homologies*). One member of the audience simply didn't want to hear it and kept offering alternative ways to see the text. I did not reject those alternative ways—most texts can be seen in more than one way—but I came to the conclusion that this member of my audience, this reader, simply didn't want to hear about racial issues. He didn't want to dance. That's all right, but he missed a good time out there on the floor, gliding around and taking steps he might never have taken otherwise.

Why didn't that audience member just give it up and try, for once? I think it was because close reading and criticism invite people to see some part of the world differently, and that is risky. If it is a really important part of the world, as racial issues usually are, then it can be risky for a reader to give him- or herself up to the critic, even for a moment. People often do not like to see the world differently and so will not embrace theories and methods that invite them to do just that. Come to think of it, I was taking a risk, too, in presenting my views to a potentially hostile, or at least unwilling, person. As a critic, one also risks that the reader will not understand or even try to, will disagree, will reject one's theories and methods, will disagree with one's findings, and so forth. Good, critical close reading involves risk for both critic and reader.

When we ask others to risk something, when we risk something ourselves, lives can be affected in ways large and small. The mutual-fund director who invites people to invest in his fund has great potential to affect people's lives financially. The religious thinker who proposes a new way of thinking about spirituality has the potential to affect lives powerfully. When some dimension of our lives is on the line, then ethics, or rules and considerations that guide our conduct, come into play. For that reason, *close reading that involves theories and methods always has an ethical dimension.* We must think about the ethical effects both of asking people to see the world in a certain way and of doing so ourselves, as we apply theories and methods in critical close reading. Suppose your reader accepts your reading; you have changed the way that reader looks at one text and perhaps at a great many more texts.

It is beyond the scope of this book to say what your ethics should be. That depends on many personal, cultural, and spiritual factors. But I do urge all of you to take responsibility for how you share your close readings with others and to see that the job of critical close reading is not only for your own self-enrichment. Critical close reading is a social, and therefore an ethical, responsibility.

❖ WORKING WITH THEORIES AND METHODS

Let's turn to a particular theory as a working example. In several books, the great multidisciplinary twentieth-century scholar Kenneth Burke developed theories that many have found useful. I will not attempt to say whether he has just one grand theory or several of them, for Burkean scholarship has disagreed on that point. But I believe one could sum up this theory from across many of his works: *Human thoughts and motivations are formed in language or other symbolic systems. What we say and how we say it generates our motives more than it reflects our motives. Language is a system of signs that molds systems of motives. What language does on a page or in a speaker's utterances will mold in some way what the readers and listeners of those texts think and do. We can study the characteristics of language to deduce the characteristic motivations of those who use that language. Likewise, if you want to change what people do and think, change their language.*

Now, clearly this theory is a generalization that goes beyond particular, isolated cases. It is not a statement about what last night's speech by the president does; it is a statement about what all speeches, essays, conversations, letters, and so forth, do. The theory also has a coherent rationale; it is held together by a central vision of how the human mind works through symbol systems. The theory is broadly applicable and useful. It says that if you want to know how racism works, you must examine racist language. If you want to change gender stereotyping, then change how we write about gender. The theory can be disproved and disagreed with, since someone might reasonably take the stance that our thoughts and motives are formed by physical experience or by the chemical workings of the brain and reflected in language, rather than being generated by language. The theory can also be supported, and it has been, through hundreds, if not thousands, of critical studies that use Burkean ideas. If you want to track some of these studies down, the online *KB Journal* (http://www.kbjournal.org/) is a good place to start.

Just looking at that theory by itself, you may feel unprepared to use it in a close reading. That would be a reasonable reaction on your part. I have not yet talked about methods and techniques, which are the ways we connect theories to texts. Let's turn to those aids to close reading now. We'll come back to working with this Burkean theory in a moment.

❖ HALFWAY DOWN, DEDUCTIVELY:
   METHODS AND TECHNIQUES

Methods are suggested by theories. A theory explains how the world is; a method tells you how to act in the world described by the theory. A *method* is a *systematic way to act to change the world, to perform more effectively in life, or to gain more knowledge about it.* You can also think of a method as *a system of techniques.* Think of method as a concept that organizes certain specific techniques together for more effective knowledge and action. *The method is the plan for thinking and action, and the techniques are the embodied actions or ways of thinking that achieve the plan.* Methods and the techniques suggested by method are very practical; they are ways for us to be effective in the world.

We use methods and techniques all the time. You may have a method for sewing a garment, and if you think about it, you will realize that it is composed of lots of techniques—for threading the bobbin, laying out the pattern, basting seams, stitching hems, and so forth. You may have a method for getting a crying infant to sleep, and it involves several techniques that are specific ways to hold it, rock it, feed it, burp it, and so on. You may have a method for building a set of shelves that involves techniques of sawing wood, driving screws, squaring joints, and the like.

Let's give some thought to how methods connect theories to the world. First, we need to realize that *methods are ways of applying theories.* We learned that a theory is a system of thought that asserts some regularities in experience. A theory tells us that some part of the world regularly and reliably operates thus and so. A method, being a systematic way to look at that part of the world, is a way to link up the theory with the world, to detect whether the theory is operating in any particular case and to show how it might be doing so. A method might tell you to look for systematic patterns across different kinds of texts. But the theory that grounds that method might tell you that *all texts are embodiments of a wide, but not an infinite, variety of formal patterns,* and that those patterns have a great deal to do with audience expectations and reactions. Several theories take that position: Campbell and Jamieson's genre theory and many of the theories of the rhetorician Kenneth Burke are examples. These theories go with slightly different methods that tell the critic what to look for in real texts.

Let's turn to an example of methods and their relationship to theory. You will recall that we used Kenneth Burke's theory earlier as a general illustration of what theories do. Burke, you remember, developed the theory that motivations follow from language use. Now, what method did Burke suggest that enables us to use that theory as we travel through the strange land of a new text? How can we apply that general theory to actual texts?

Burke developed quite a few methods, but let us take his pentad as an example, a concept he explained in greatest detail in his book *A Grammar of Motives* (xv). Burke's method hinges on a metaphor of drama. His dramatistic method says that language motivates people to think of the world as if it were a dramatic production. Of course, any dramatic production has several dimensions; just think of all the different things you see and experience when you watch a play or a film. Burke's pentadic method says that we can detect and organize the ways in which language motivates people if we think dramatistically. The pentad has five parts: *act*, the kinds of things that are done; *agent*, the person or group that does the action; *agency*, the means by which action is performed; *scene,* the context in which the action takes place; and *purpose,* the underlying reasons, goals, or philosophies that guide action.

Different plays and different moments in plays will stress one or a combination of these five terms over the others. A play may emphasize act (that one fatal misstep, the unforgivable remark). One play may focus on agents (interesting characters, famous people, the saint, the person "born bad"). Another may stress scene (out in the country, during a war, in an economic depression). Another may emphasize agency (nobody has enough money, everybody has too much money). A play may stress purpose (religious or morality plays). Burke argues that ordinary language may be understood as if it were stressing one or a combination of these five terms. Examine language, he said, to see which of the terms is emphasized. That will tell you how people are motivated by that language, he said. If a person speaks constantly as if the scene made the world the way it is, for example, that person might be much less motivated by personal responsibility than is another person whose language emphasizes the importance of agents in life. Many Burkean studies have been done using the pentadic method. For instance, see my essay "A Pentadic Analysis. . . ." in the References.

If we look at well-known lines from some famous books, poems, plays, songs, or sayings, we can see language that stresses one of the terms of the pentad, language that seems to suggest that the audience adopt motives based on act, agent, agency, scene, or purpose. Here are some:

- Act: *"Two roads diverged in a wood, and I—*
  I took the one less traveled by,
  And that has made all the difference."

  (Robert Frost, "The Road Not Taken")

- Agent: "Marley was dead: to begin with. There is no doubt whatever about that. The register of his burial was signed by the clergyman, the clerk, the undertaker, and the chief mourner. Scrooge signed it: and Scrooge's name was good upon 'Change, for anything he chose to put his hand to. Old Marley was as dead as a door-nail." (Charles Dickens, *A Christmas Carol*)

- Agency: "Oh, if you ain't got the do re mi, folks, you ain't got the do re mi, Why, you better go back to beautiful Texas, Oklahoma, Kansas, Georgia, Tennessee." (Woody Guthrie, "If You Ain't Got The Do Re Mi")

- Scene: "*It was a dark and stormy night*; the rain fell in torrents—except at occasional intervals, when it was checked by a violent gust of wind which swept up the streets (for it is in London that our scene lies), rattling along the housetops, and fiercely agitating the scanty flame of the lamps that struggled against the darkness." (Edward George Bulwer-Lytton, *Paul Clifford*)

- Purpose: "If I speak in the tongues of men and of angels, but have not love, I am a noisy gong or a clanging cymbal. And if I have prophetic powers, and understand all mysteries and all knowledge, and if I have all faith, so as to remove mountains, but have not love, I am nothing." (St. Paul, I Corinthians 13:1–3)

In the example for act, the act of taking one road and not another changed the speaker's world and "has made all the difference." Dickens sets up a proper ghost story by emphasizing the character of the agent, Marley, who shortly floats disembodied through Scrooge's bedroom door, and tells us a little about Scrooge as an agent as well. One of the best-known agencies is money, or "dough," humorously referred to as "the do re mi" in Woody Guthrie's Depression-era song, in which he claims that without that agency you'd do just as well to give it up and go back to beautiful Texas. Bulwer-Lytton's Victorian melodrama describes all sorts of creepy and mysterious goings-on that are perfectly in tune with the scene of a dark and stormy night. And St. Paul features purpose, in this case the guiding purpose of love, as more important than any action or feature of agents.

Now, this book is not about Burke's pentad, but think about how well equipped you, the close reader, would be to see his theory—that language generates motives—if you had in hand this pentadic method, which calls your attention to certain kinds of motives that are generated by certain kinds of language. Think further about how such a combination of theory and method might help you in a close reading of these texts. Most people have read or seen a film of *A Christmas Carol.* These agent-centered opening statements actually continue through the whole story, do they not? Doesn't *A Christmas Carol* tell us that the kind of person you are is what makes all the difference? We see how Scrooge's agent, his being and personality, is changed, and with that change of agent comes a whole range of transformation in other agents as well as in the acts he undertakes. Scenes are changed once Scrooge is changed. So the pentadic method might suggest that you look for a focus on agent-centered motives in the book, and that would indeed be a fruitful way to read it.

EXERCISE 2.2

Let's get a little practice using this particular method of the pentad. Remember, we are using this method to notice ways in which, as Burke's theory claims, language generates motives. You might do that in several ways:

❖ Get several examples of hip-hop and find songs that seem to feature one term or another. This is not at all hard to do for as rich and varied a discourse as hip-hop. Hint: How many songs say that the people of this town or that town are motivated and shaped by the nature of the town itself (scene)? How many hip-hop songs celebrate all the outlaw things that the singer does (act) or is (agent)?

❖ Take the long-term view, and look at a television series that has been shown for a long time. Looking at this discourse over the long haul, does it consistently and repeatedly seem to suggest that the world is the way it is due to one or a combination of the pentadic terms? Hint: How would the *Law and Order* series of shows differ if set in a different scene, say, the Old West?

❖ Think about different categories or genres of television shows, and think about whether some of those genres seem to center around a term of the pentad. Take makeover and style shows, for instance (*What Not to Wear, Project Runway, How Do I Look?*). Are they keyed to one of the pentadic terms? How about reality shows? Sports broadcasts?

Let's do another exercise in using theory and method, but in this case I'm going to leave you more on your own. Media scholar David Altheide observed in 1985—and, let's recall, this was relatively early in the age of personal computing devices—that an increasingly dominant medium in our technological world was the keyboard (97). Altheide observed that, increasingly, we access information, make things happen, and entertain ourselves by pecking away at something with our fingertips. You and I might think that many different media or technologies all use keyboards (stop to think about them: computers, cell phones, personal digital assistants, microwaves, blenders, television remote controls, and on and on). But Altheide had the insight to see that a unifying constant across all these applications was the need to train ourselves to interact with the world through our fingertips. Our personal and social ways of thinking about the world, he argued, are becoming shaped by the ubiquitous ease and speed of keyboards.

Key to Altheide's theory is that he argues that society, all of us, are thinking differently because of how we use keyboards, understood as a kind of medium. We come to organize life around easy access through manipulation of the fingers. A society that gets things done, that acquires knowledge, in this way may develop a short time frame of thought or action, since pecking with fingers is quick. Such a society may come to expect everything to be done easily because it is so easy to press buttons. You might want to read more about Altheide's fascinating theory and the way the keyboard influences our thought. Then let's use that idea in the following exercise.

EXERCISE 2.3

❖ Be sure you understand Altheide's theory. Reading his book will help. On your own or in groups, write approximately a page summarizing the theory. If you want to check on your statement of his theory, use our characteristics of theory from page 32; make sure your summary of Altheide's work contains *generalizations* that constitute a *coherent rationale* for how some part of the world works, that what you have written seems *broadly applicable and useful,* and that what you have written can be both *disproved* and *supported* with specific evidence from experience.

❖ Now, your task is to use Altheide's theory to help explain how some part of our experience works. So the next step is to develop some *methods* for how we go about seeing keyboards and the ways they work. Don't take the easy route and just say, "Well, they must look like a computer keyboard." Clearly, Altheide wants us to think more broadly than that. Please develop some methods that would allow you to "find" keyboards in experiences and technologies that you might not have thought of before as keyboardlike.

❖ Now, apply your methods! Be able to show how some experience, some instrument, technology, machine, or tool, works like a keyboard in Altheide's sense. Say why it is important to be able to identify that experience as a keyboard. Share the application of your methods with others in your class.

The *Zits* cartoon (Figure 2.1) may be taken as an illustration of, or even a warning about, the effects of keyboards on society. The young people in the comic are all accessing keyboards. The contorted positions of their hands even exaggerate Altheide's point—the hands and fingers seem to be doing all the work here. Contrast this younger

Figure 2.1

To view this image in full resolution, please visit www.sagepub.com/brummettstudy.

generation with the parents, who are not engaged in keyboarding, and you can read the cartoon as a commentary on the situation Altheide describes.

It's possible that you don't feel very skilled at reading these texts using Burke's theory, the pentadic method, Altheide's theory, and the methods you've devised yourself—and that's all right. Maybe these are not theories and methods to which you are attuned. Possibly, you feel that you are still not equipped to *see* texts well, to notice what is going on in them. You may not yet feel quite able to connect with the details of a text to read it closely. You need techniques.

But I'm not going to give you techniques in this chapter; that's what the rest of the book is for. Here, I just want to orient you toward what we will learn from here on out. By focusing on techniques, we will focus on the most broadly applicable, widely used tools you have in critical close reading. Techniques are shared across many theories and methods.

You might think about theories, methods, and techniques using the metaphor of friendliness. Theories tend not to be very friendly: they want to explain the world their way, and they don't often hang out with those theories over there. Theories usually suggest specific methods, but methods are often shared across theories. Methods are therefore a little "friendlier": they don't mind going to visit the other theories in the neighborhood. You might have studied some theories of attitude change, for instance, that use *statistical methods,* and, of course, statistical methods are widely shared across the social sciences. So, although methods are connected to theories, they are often found widely across theories.

Techniques are even friendlier and are widely used across theories and methods. They are widely transferable to different tasks and purposes of close reading. Techniques are quite sociable and are eager to hang out with all kinds of theories and methods. Techniques are therefore widely shared across different kinds of close readings. And that brings me to this important point: *By learning techniques of close reading, you learn ways to employ many different kinds of theories and methods.*

Techniques are specific, grounded ways to read texts closely. They are as "on the ground" as they can be and at the other end of the abstraction continuum from theory. You will recall that we started with a map metaphor, seeing theory as the map of a territory and methods as the kind of vehicle you would use to get around in the territory. A technique is the specific, applied way you would use such a vehicle in the territory.

❖ HEADING BACK UP AGAIN, INDUCTIVELY: FROM TECHNIQUES TO THEORY

I said earlier that you do not have to follow the deductive method we have been pursuing here; in fact, many critical close readers do not. Some explorers just go to a new territory to see what is there, building up their maps and their sense of the best way to get around by being in the territory. Similarly, many close readers just jump into a text and perhaps later pull together methods or theories that they believe might help others read similar texts. But I believe that *nobody explores a territory or a text without techniques.* You may not know that you have command of techniques, but you use them nevertheless—or else you stall hopelessly and never figure out the text or the territory. This implies that you can explore a territory better if you go in with some techniques—you can paddle your canoe better if you learn canoe-paddling techniques. You can hike better if you learn which shoes are right for the terrain and for your feet. And you are better able to read a text closely and critically if you learn some techniques. That's what you'll do in the rest of the book.

Having climbed down the ladder from theory to method to technique, let me point you in the direction of the inductive process of building up from technique to theory. Most of this you will need to do yourself if you decide to create theories and methods, because that's what the inductive method is: using what you have found to generate the generalizations of theory and its methods. I'll just point you in that direction because this really isn't a book on theory building. But let me stress again that the inductive approach is a perfectly legitimate, frequently used approach to critical close reading. To show you what I mean by pointing you in the direction of inductive thinking, let's do a short exercise.

EXERCISE 2.4

❖ Let's start by posing a question: How do television shows begin? All inductive thinking begins with questions like this one, with a sense of curiosity and perhaps a sense that some useful generalizations might be made. Often such questions lead to other questions: Do different kinds of shows begin in regular, predictable ways? Does the way the show begins affect how it closes? And so forth.

❖ How would you go about answering such a set of questions? You will need to march right into the territory: go look at some television shows! Depending on your questions, you may need to watch several. You should observe closely and take notes on how different kinds of shows begin, at the very least.

❖ Be self-reflective as you watch these shows and take notes. You are using techniques, whether you know it or not. How are you allowing yourself to determine what "counts" as the beginning of a show? Or the end of a show? What do you take notes of? In what form do you take them? What do you note down and what do you not? What technologies do you use? Answers to these and other questions will show you that you are not flailing around wildly but are, in fact, using techniques. You could even write your own paper titled "Techniques for Observing Beginnings and Endings of Television Shows." You might observe with others (which is also a kind of technique) so you can compare notes.

❖ Now, gather the evidence you have gleaned, and think about what generalizations you can make about how television shows begin. Have any patterns emerged? Are you able to say that most or all news shows begin one way, that most or all sports broadcasts start another way? What do you think it means, what effect does this have on the viewing audience, that they begin one way or another? Now, you are moving toward theory. If you have found some regularities, then what you end up saying about theory will have those characteristics of theory: generalizability, coherent rationale, broad applicability and utility, the ability to be disproved and also supported.

❖ At the same time you are moving up the inductive ladder to form theory, you will likely be forming some methods. If someone came to you and said, "All right, I want to know how I can apply your theory and study the ways that television shows (or films or plays or country-western songs) begin," how would you tell them to proceed? Your descriptions of how to apply your theory to these texts will likely be kinds of methods.

To move inductively, however, it helps to know techniques first, and that is where we are now headed, to review a number of widely applicable, useful techniques for reading a text critically. The rest of this book will look at a wide range of these "friendly" techniques that are widely applicable across many theories and methods.

❖ SUMMARY AND LOOKING AHEAD

In this chapter we have studied the connections among theories, methods, techniques, and close reading. We learned that *theories, methods, and techniques are ways to figure out the real world.* In close reading, they provide the structure that allows for a disciplined reading of texts.

Using a map metaphor, you learned that theories are like maps to territories, methods are how to move about in those territories, and techniques are the specific ways one does that moving about. In close reading, we use theories, methods, and techniques to move around texts rather than territories. You also learned that there are two general approaches to using theories, methods, and techniques. First, there is a *deductive*, or "top-down," method, in which one is guided by an existing theory and its methods, and one uses techniques to read a text in ways suggested by theory. Second, there is an *inductive*, or "bottom-up," method in which one uses techniques to explore a text freely, allowing generalizations to emerge that may eventually form theories and methods. Both are legitimate and useful ways to engage in critical close reading.

Theories are widely available from many different sources. Students already will have been exposed to theories that can be useful in close reading. You learned to recognize theories by their characteristics: they are *generalizations* that offer a *coherent rationale* of how some part of the world works and in that way are *broadly useful and applicable*. A theory may be *disproved* if objects or events in the world consistently disagree with it, but a theory may also be *supported* by evidence that confirms its generalizations.

A theory leads to knowledge by providing a kind of *translation*, by urging its user to see something in the world in terms of something else. By seeing a political advertisement in terms of a theory of political persuasion, for instance, we arrive at knowledge of the world. Therefore, in proposing a theory and its methods for observation, the critic is offering a new way to see the world. That is *risky* for both the critic and the reader, and we learned that such risk means that critical close reading always has *ethical* implications. Both reader and critic surrender some amount of control and familiarity in agreeing to explore a text together using theory and methods.

Turning our attention to methods and techniques, we learned that *method is the plan for thinking and action, and techniques are the embodied actions that achieve the plan.* We used Kenneth Burke's dramatistic theory and his pentadic method as an illustration of how those concepts work. The reader was also invited to investigate David Altheide's theory of keyboards and to apply that theory to texts as another illustration of how theories and methods guide us in critical close reading.

The *inductive method* begins with techniques of closely reading texts. We considered the question of how television shows begin and end, and you were invited to read several shows closely and work inductively to move toward some generalizations. Along the way, you will have formulated some methods for applying your theory in the future. You also discovered that techniques are widely applicable across many theories and methods.

It is now time to turn our attention to techniques, which will occupy us for the rest of the book. One group of techniques is keyed to *form*, and that is the subject of Chapter 3. Another group of techniques is attuned to the idea of *transformations*, which we discuss in Chapter 4. Finally, in Chapter 5 we look at techniques based on the idea of *argument*.

3

Using Form for Close Reading

❖ ❖ ❖

O ne of the most useful techniques of close reading, one used across a wide range of theories and methods, is the detection of form. What do I mean by *form*? Form is *the structure, or pattern, that organizes a text.* Form is always part of our thinking and living. You can see its presence in your life by considering a few examples.

Most of you have a song or two that is your current favorite. How many times in a row could you stand to listen to that song? Could you stand to hear it now? I'm guessing that most of you would certainly be glad to hear it again right now and probably more than once. Let's think about how strange that really is. You aren't going to learn anything new from the song. Whatever story it tells, whatever claims of lost love or broken hearts it makes, you already know about. You aren't really going to get any new information from the song. So what do you gain by hearing it again?

The reason you can hear the song over and over again is that music is highly *formal.* Form—pattern, structure—is essential to music. Rhythm is a kind of pattern; harmony or chordal structures are forms. You can hear your favorite song over and over because when you hear it you are largely experiencing the forms within the music. People like to follow forms in music as well as in literature, television shows, film, and so forth. Form is an itch we never tire of scratching, so repetition is less likely to reduce its appeal.

In contrast, suppose you ask someone for a telephone number. Your friend repeats it a couple of times; you memorize it and thank your friend, saying you've "got it." Now, how many times could you stand to hear that telephone number repeated? Were your friend to keep saying it over and over, you'd probably ask him or her forcefully to stop—you might even worry about your friend's health. Why is it that you can you hear your favorite song over and over, but once you get the telephone number, you don't need to hear it any more?

You can think of every message you receive as having both *form* and *content*. Form is the *pattern* the message follows. Content is the *information*, the facts or news, that the message contains. If you want to send congratulations to a friend on a promotion at work, for instance, you can send pretty much the same content or information through the different forms of a letter, a poem, an e-mail, a text message, or a casual conversation. Notice that the patterns of letters, poems, e-mail, texting, and conversations are different. They follow different "rules" of production and consumption, and the rules constitute the form of each method. Furthermore, note that although the content or information of the message is brand new (your friend has never before received this particular promotion), the form or pattern of letter, poem, e-mail, texting, or conversation is familiar. We all know how letters "work," while each new letter conveys new information. That, in fact, is an important characteristic of form: it follows familiar patterns that are widely understood within a culture. Form usually appeals to people the most when it is familiar, but content or information usually appeals to people the most when it is new and unfamiliar.

Your favorite song contains some information, but that's rarely why we listen to songs—to get the news. And a telephone number usually follows a pattern; note that when we give someone a phone number, we usually pause right after the first three numbers to match the dash that is inserted there when the number is written down. That's a pattern for ordering and remembering a phone number. But when we experience a song, we are experiencing patterns much more, and when we learn a telephone number, we are experiencing content much more. Both are important; you couldn't live without either one. Both are inseparable; it would be difficult to find any text without both form and content, and they are also continuous with each other in that pattern usually gives you information, and information usually is patterned.

Notice the connection between form and the pleasurable experience of hearing that song. *Form moves people more than content does.* Our minds like to follow patterns; we seek them out to help us think about how to live in the world. For that reason, form has more to do with rhetorical effect than content does because it is usually form that gets and holds people's interest, attention, and participation in a text.

You can remind yourself of the power of form if you think about mnemonic devices. *A mnemonic device is a trick you use to help you memorize something.* You know how helpful that is in studying for tests, in remembering the content of crucial information you will need, and so forth. Now, suppose you are taking a class in British history and you are asked to memorize the royal houses (or dynasties) of England. If you just try to memorize the names Norman, Plantagenet, Lancaster, York, Tudor, Stuart, Hanover, and Windsor, you are grappling mainly with content or information not ordered by a form, and it may be difficult to learn. But if you can link that information to a form, it's much easier to learn. One form is any common English sentence. Sentences follow patterns; they develop a thought along a form and so are easier to remember than are seemingly random words. If you can remember "No plan like yours to study history wisely," then you can learn the royal houses of England, in order! Because, of course, each word of the sentence begins with the same letter as the royal house, taken in order: N, P, L, Y, T, S, H, W. By the same token, we used to be able to remember the order of the planets in order of their distances from the Sun (Mercury, Venus, Earth, Mars, Jupiter, Saturn, Uranus, Neptune, Pluto) by remembering the far easier sentence "My very earnest mother just served us nine pizzas," but then astronomers dropped Pluto from the list of planets, so now we will have to recast the sentence.

While this chapter will focus on form, and form tends to emerge in many texts across time and space, let me remind you of the importance of historical and textual context, as we discussed in Chapter 1. It remains vital to read texts in their contexts. But in this chapter, we turn our attention to ways to read the forms of texts that cut across contexts.

The point of this introduction has been to emphasize the importance of form in explaining what people find attractive in texts. Therefore, form is an important part of the rhetoric of texts, and a rhetorical, critical close reading of texts needs to develop techniques for studying form. These are ways to see form better, ways to notice form more clearly. I have organized the rest of this chapter around three techniques of studying form: attention to *narrative, genre,* and *persona.*

❖ NARRATIVE

A story, or narrative, is more form than content. Form is what turns a group of random facts into a story. A newspaper reporter gathers a lot of facts but doesn't write the story until the facts are put in order—into a form called a story. Historians spend hours examining bits and pieces of evidence in museums, libraries, and archives and then put those bits and pieces into histories, which are actually stories about African empires, Japanese warriors, Theodore Roosevelt, and so forth. In reading the stories in books, on television, and in movies, we are enjoying their forms. In this book, I refer to this formal nature of stories as *narrative* because we will find narrative, or storylike, patterns in texts that seem not to be the usual "once upon a time" type of story. To see how narrative and form are closely connected, let's do an exercise.

EXERCISE 3.1

❖ Consider this set of sentences: (1) The river people vowed revenge upon the mountain people. (2) It was pleasant and easy living by the river. (3) Once upon a time, two groups of people lived within a few miles of each other: the river people and the mountain people. (4) There was much killing and slaughter. (5) Therefore, a war party was formed to go up into the mountains. (6) The mountain people were jealous of this and planned a raid to steal some property from the river people. (7) Surrounding the mountain village, the river people attacked. (8) In the dark of night, the mountain people crept down to the river village and carried away much livestock and property. (9) The river people had triumphed after all.

❖ Not a well-organized group of sentences, is it? It really is just a random collection of bits of information. Yet think about how your mind is struggling to impose some kind of order or pattern to make sense of those sentences. Don't you have a feeling that some sentences must go before and some must go after? Narrative is like a powerful force pushing to assert itself in texts. That random group of sentences in some way wants to become patterned, and when it is patterned, it will become a narrative. Pattern is essential to narrative.

❖ Now, first on your own and then in groups, arrange those sentences so they make sense. I'm guessing it is likely that most people will find the same narrative pattern or order that makes sense of that mishmash of sentences.

It's clear that the sentences in Exercise 3.1 are part of a story. But not all texts are obviously stories. Therefore, you may be wondering why we are looking for narrative in texts that may not be stories. The answer is that story and pattern are much the same thing, the one is the essence of the other, and *most texts contain storylike forms, or narratives, to some extent.* Not all texts are stories or narratives. Even if a text is not explicitly a story, it will likely contain elements of story, or narrative. In close reading, narrative is more a method used by the critic than a statement about the text. Looking for what is storylike about a text helps us to see its form. Therefore, *most texts can be read closely by looking for elements of narrative in them. Most texts can be better understood if we look for the elements of narrative within them.* We will study those elements of narrative more carefully, but let's do another exercise designed to show you that narrative is more common than you think in texts that may not seem like stories.

EXERCISE 3.2

❖   Think about a cowboy boot. Imagine just seeing a plain photograph of one in a magazine or movie. I'll bet it's hard to think about a cowboy boot without a narrative starting to form. Maybe it's a story from a movie or TV show you've seen, or maybe it's a story suggested by someone you know who wears boots. *Most of the ordinary objects and actions we might encounter in texts and images imply narratives.* What are some bits and pieces of story that start to pop into your head when you think about cowboy boots? How do those pieces of stories change as you change from one image of a boot to another (an old, broken-in boot, a boot encrusted with rhinestones, a child's boot, a bright-red boot with leather tassels)?

- Please look at Figure 3.1. You might not think of a magazine ad as being a narrative, but here is the skeleton of a narrative in the advertisement. Notice how the reader is invited to contribute to that narrative, to fill in details (conceiving a child?!) that the bits and pieces of narrative here do not provide. Many texts do this. Think of some other examples of texts that seem not to be narratives but that include narrative elements suggesting more-developed stories.

- Please look at Figure 3.2. There is even less explicit narrative here than in Figure 3.1, but a narrative struggles to the surface

Figure 3.1

To view this image in full resolution, please visit www.sagepub.com/brummettstudy.

Figure 3.2

To view this image in full resolution, please visit www.sagepub.com/brummettstudy.

here, too, does it not? What story is told by the two pairs of cowboy boots, one large and one small?

- Reflect on the rhetorical value of the narrative bits and pieces in
  both Figure 3.1 and Figure 3.2. How much of the appeal of each
  ad, how much of your interest and involvement, is created by
  the little "hooks" of story that are provided by the texts? Or, to
  think of it another way, how much of the text is revealed in a
  close reading when you start *looking* for narrative?

When I refer to *elements of narrative*, I am referring to what it is
about a story that makes it a story. But I am also referring to *elements of
any text*, whether literally a story or not, *that create form or pattern in the
text*. No text goes unpatterned, and therefore every text will contain
elements of pattern or form that are the essence of narrative. Three elements of narrative are especially useful in critical close readings: *coherence and sequence, tension and resolution*, and *alignment and opposition*.

Coherence and Sequence

In thinking about the narrative forms of stories or movies, you realize that what happens must hold together and make sense (coherence),
and it must "move" or "get somewhere" (sequence). Coherence and
sequence are both important principles of form in general, and their
centrality to stories helps us see how closely related are form and narrative. For instance, often red why and could sure so Doctor under
springtime Philadelphia hectic. Now, what just happened? I offered a
string of words that did not make sense (they were not coherent) and
did not move recognizably from one place to another, from one
thought, emotion, or idea to another (sequence). You have been able to
read every other sentence I've written in this book (I hope) because
I put the words of the other sentences into a coherent sequence. These
principles underlie successful narratives in every form. Perhaps you
have turned off a television show or quit reading a book because you
couldn't make heads or tails of what was going on, and you really
didn't care what came next. I'm guessing the show or book had little
coherence and sequence. But on the other hand, if you have experienced a movie or a sporting event where you were never distracted,
your attention was completely absorbed, and you were on the edge of
your seat from start to finish, then you encountered a text with a lot of
coherence and sequence. These elements of narrative tell us a lot about
the overall meanings and the effects offered by texts, so we should pay
attention to them in close readings.

Coherence and sequence are elements of narrative that prompt the critical close reader to ask the following questions about the text.

- *Coherence:* What overall theme, effect, tone, or meaning is created by this text? Are there several overall themes, effects, tones, and meanings that an audience might plausibly find here, and if so, how does the text support those different coherences? If there are serious contradictions or incoherences in the text, should they be considered flaws in the text, or do they add to the rhetorical effect of the text? How much does the text need the reader to help provide coherence—in other words, is the text clearly and strongly coherent, or must the reader work extra hard to pull together the theme, effect, tone, or meaning offered by the text?

- *Sequence:* Does the stream of words, signs, images, and events in the text flow logically and naturally from one point to the next? What kind of expectations does the text develop early in the minds of the reader, and are those expectations fulfilled or not? Does the text ever develop in a different direction from the one it seems to promise at some point? If the text is powerfully and clearly sequential, if it flows naturally and clearly from one state to the next, is the text for that reason boring, predictable, and uninteresting—or is it powerful? If the text changes direction and surprises the audience, violating expectations, is the text for that reason nonsensical and frustrating—or is it interesting and edgy?

(EXERCISE 3.3)

Let us do a quick close reading of a film that is by now considered a classic of horror or supernatural movies, *The Sixth Sense.* If you have not seen the film yet, go see it before proceeding! Be warned—I am about to give away the "surprise" ending. Much of the rhetorical effect of this movie has to do with coherence and sequence, and asking some of the questions in the previous paragraph can help us understand what the film does to achieve those effects.

❖   Notice the extent to which a shift in coherence is key to the surprise ending. The audience is encouraged throughout the film to see the nine-year-old boy, Cole, as troubled or haunted. We are also encouraged by the film to see Dr. Crowe, the child psychiatrist, as dedicated to his work and to healing young Cole. Think about which components of the film encourage that way of making sense, or creating coherence, in the movie. Now think about the surprising shift at the end of the film, in which we discover that Dr. Crowe has himself been a ghost all along, haunting the boy along with all the other spirits. Notice how the way we have put the text together in our heads must shift radically because of that discovery. You might note that the film shifts from one coherence to another, rather than simply becoming incoherent. Now, on your own or in a group, use some of the questions listed earlier to explain why this shift is rhetorically successful (the film was an instant popular success and is still considered a classic). Think of more recent films, novels, or television shows that had similarly successful surprise endings, and explain why the shift in coherence worked well. Also, think of some texts where such a shift did not work but created confusion, and use the same questions to explain why.

❖ How does the sequentiality of *The Sixth Sense* work with coherence to point the audience in one direction and then to change directions radically? Think about the progressions of scenes—what the director shows and does not show us. How do the inclusion of some events and the exclusion of others create a sequence that leads to surprise? (For instance, it's obvious that showing Dr. Crowe's funeral shortly after he is shot early in the film would give the whole secret away.) How does careful patterning of one event and image after another preserve the secret ending until the final reversal?

❖ The director of the film, M. Night Shyamalan, is well known for films with surprise twists and turns. See his film *The Village*, for instance. Do a critical close reading of those texts or others you think are interesting because of what they do with coherence and sequence.

Tension and Resolution

We can think of tension and resolution as elements of narrative following from coherence and sequence. A good story will create some kind of tension in the minds of the audience. There are many different sorts of tension that can be created. There might be a mystery to be solved (Who killed the countess?). There might be a problem of love to settle (Bob loves Heather, but Heather loves Amy, but Amy loves Bob). The tension may have to do with triumph or defeat (Who will win the state championship game? Will the evil Nazi scientist be kidnapped?). The tension might also be one of emotions or aesthetic reactions that cannot be put into words: imagine hearing your favorite song and then stopping your MP3 player just as the song is about to go into the bridge or the chorus. Don't you have a feeling of incompleteness, of "needing" the music to continue, of being left hanging? That feeling is the tension the song creates aesthetically and emotionally.

Texts will then address that tension. Often, the tension will be resolved. The most typical example of that is the happy ending. Sometimes the tension is allowed to remain, as is the case in some recent experimental music or in some films where the purpose is to leave the audience in an unsettled state of mind. Films that are clearly made with the possibility of a sequel will often not resolve tensions adequately. For instance, the first two films in *The Lord of the Rings* series paralleled the original books in leaving many issues up in the air and unresolved. The first installment of the *Pirates of the Caribbean* series, *Curse of the Black Pearl*, resolved its tensions pretty well because nobody knew, when it was being made, whether it would be a success. It was, and therefore the second film, *Dead Man's Chest*, has practically no resolution of tension at all; the producers of the film were confident that audiences would want to see the third installment to see how it all worked out. In television, soap operas or daytime dramas are masters of tension and resolution: each episode creates enough tension to keep the audience interested and motivated to continue watching, while each issue also resolves enough tension to satisfy the audience and keep frustration at a minimum. Clearly, a tension created and then resolved or not is a matter of overall coherence in a text, and how a tension might first be created and then resolved, perhaps more than once in a text, is a matter of sequencing.

The critical close reader can use the ideas of tension and resolution to explore how a text might move its audience. Think of the audience's state of mind and feeling at the end of experiencing a text as the rhetorical effect created, and think of the extent to which arousal and satisfaction of tensions or lack thereof are part of that state of mind and feeling. What does it mean, and what does it move an audience to do, think, or feel, that certain tensions were created and then resolved or not?—these questions can be asked of texts.

EXERCISE 3.4

If we think about sequencing as something that requires a text that moves or changes in time, such as a song or film, we may also think about tension and resolution as requiring such a text—don't you need a "before" and an "after" to create tensions and then address them? In this exercise, let us look at a "still" text, a magazine ad. It is important to realize that readers, even as they engage texts such as this one that do not move in time, nevertheless experience sequence and coherence. Figure 3.3 shows us how a text that stands still can also create and then resolve tensions.

Figure 3.3

To view this image in full resolution, please visit www.sagepub.com/brummettstudy.

❖ Look at the image in the advertisement. A narrative is certainly suggested here. What kind of story might a reader plausibly attribute to the image of the vehicle pulling the camper up the hill? What will happen in the next day or two? Think about how such a story involves expectation or anticipation: What should you look forward to in such a story? What adventures or good times might be coming? Now, think about how such pleasant tensions might be resolved. Might the reader plausibly be left with a desire to experience those adventures? And isn't the desire to resolve that exciting tension part of the logic of the advertisement, a desire to purchase a vehicle like the one shown?

❖ Read the fine print at the top of the advertisement. What kind of tension is created here? Think about how that text creates the desire

(Continued)

(Continued)

or anticipation of dominating others, of showing one's superiority, of displaying masculinity. How would that tension or desire be resolved? Obviously, the reader will have to resolve the tension, but how does this text offer a possible resolution of the tension?

❖ Find another advertisement that creates tensions and offers resolutions. State why the creation and resolution of tension has rhetorical, persuasive power. Also, think about the creation and resolution of tensions that might go beyond the intensions of a persuader (in the case of Figure 3.3, to sell cars)—how might a text create tensions and resolutions in ways that may not have been planned consciously?

Alignment and Opposition

Being "for" and "against" things is a profoundly fundamental human trait. Even little children will draw up sides, hang out with these kids over here while opposing those kids over there. Alignment (being for) and opposition (being against) are encoded into the very structure of our language. When we speak, very often what we say implies other words, phrases, and concepts that "go with" or "go against" what we have to say. Such alignment and opposition vary depending on how the text organizes its component signs. If I speak of "black," that may imply an opposition to "white." But if I speak of "black, white, orange, purple, golden, and red," then we think of those terms as aligned insofar as all of them are colors. To talk about "Republicans" may imply an opposition to "Democrats," unless we speak of "Republicans and Democrats" voting unanimously to condemn a terrorist action, in which case they are aligned. Most signs, whether verbal or visual, contain the potential to be in alignment with or opposition to most other signs. The critical close reader must see how this particular text orders them.

There is a great deal of rhetorical power in how alignments and oppositions are created in texts. Today, for example, many texts of news broadcasts, talk radio programs, and blogs will assert an alignment of "Islam" and "terrorists." Thirty years ago, no such alignment would have been considered; in fact, such texts might have drawn an opposition between a religious perspective like Islam and an apparently violent and immoral perspective like terrorism. Of course, this should remind us that there is no natural and necessary alignment between Islam and terrorism and that to align them—to link them together—is a rhetorical action designed to achieve particular political and social ends.

Another way to think about alignment and opposition is to say that most texts will organize signs internally so as to "pick fights" among some signs and "make friends" among others. This is the work of the text, making use of the potentials within signs. "Carrots" have, for instance, more potential to be aligned with "onions" than with "Volvos," and so most texts that speak of both will align them in that way. But I suppose it is possible that some text might align carrots with Volvos. And it is also easy to put carrots and onions in contradiction: "Would you prefer carrots or onions as your side dish?" There, they are now opposites insofar as that little text is concerned! So it is important for the critical close reader to see how a text aligns and opposes its signs.

EXERCISE 3.5

❖   One of the great haunted-house stories is Shirley Jackson's novel *The Haunting of Hill House*. It is the basis for several motion pictures and a wonderful, scary read. This is the opening paragraph: "No live organism can continue for long to exist sanely under conditions of absolute reality; even larks and katydids are supposed, by some, to dream. Hill House, not sane, stood by itself against its hills, holding darkness within; it had stood so for eighty years and might stand for eighty more. Within, walls continued upright, bricks met neatly, floors were firm, and doors were sensibly shut; silence lay steadily against the wood and stone of Hill House, and whatever walked there, walked alone."

❖   All sorts of oppositions and alignments fall into place in that paragraph. The first sentence opposes sanity to absolute reality and then puts dreaming on the side of sanity. Interesting, isn't it, that absolute reality should be positioned as a crazy way to be? Now, where is Hill House in this? Why, not sane, as we are immediately told. And then we have a breakdown of its "absolute reality" in that its component parts of walls, bricks, floors are sensible, upright, and so forth. These sensible building materials hold darkness within, and here darkness is aligned with absolute reality and insanity. Note that we are told that all this sensibility is against nature, for the paragraph says explicitly that Hill House stands against the hills around it.

(Continued)

(Continued)

Earlier we learned that larks and katydids, parts of nature, dream and are thus sane on the one hand but not sensible on the other hand. And inside Hill House, in its darkness, where walls are logically upright and brick sensibly meets brick, there is a suggestion that *something* walks. Creepy, eh? And perhaps not entirely sane. Furthermore, it walks alone, solitude being aligned with insanity inside just as Hill House itself stands by itself against its hills. Map out all these oppositions and alignments—it might be useful to draw a diagram of them.

❖ So given this original picking of fights and making of friends, what do you expect the novel will offer us, what kinds of meanings and motivations? If someone who enters Hill House is a sensible, no-nonsense individual, will that person be sane or insane? What will happen to them? If someone is a dreamer, a bit eccentric, and visits the house, where is he or she in opposition and alignment? Will the spooks get that person? What expectations are raised in just this first paragraph as to what sort of adventures might await those who enter the house?

❖ With others in your class, bring in similar pages or paragraphs and explore the oppositions and alignments created in the texts. Pay close attention to the rhetorical work done by these alignments and oppositions How might a reader be motivated to read the rest of the text or to act in life, given the way that signs are organized in the examples you study?

❖ GENRE

The idea of genre is the second main technique of identifying form that we explore in this chapter. In many ways, genre is a natural extension of narrative. Think of a genre as *a recurring type of text within a context.* In their landmark study of genre, Karlyn Kohrs Campbell and Kathleen Hall Jamieson describe a genre as a recurring kind of textual event with three components: *style, substance,* and *situation* (24). That gives us one useful scheme for identifying genres.

Take the commencement speech, for instance, which is given at college graduation exercises. The *situation* of graduation recurs; it happens over and over and is an occasion of joy and celebration. Such situations call for certain kinds of responses. For that reason, there is a genre of commencement speeches, which are given in situations like that. We expect commencement speeches to have a certain *substance,* that is, to address certain kinds of issues with certain kinds of arguments or statements (the time of preparation is behind you, your careers lie ahead, and so forth). We expect commencement speeches to have a certain *style:* joyful and light but with serious overtones as the speaker addresses the challenges that lie ahead. This does not mean that every commencement speech will have exactly the same style and substance in response to the situation of graduation—there is the comic or ironic style, there is the utterly serious substance—but every departure from the genre is judged by the expectations of the genre itself. And that is what is key to a genre: *audience expectations.* People come to a graduation expecting to hear certain kinds of texts. They may hear them and they may not, but what they hear is judged in comparison to the generic expectations.

We have many such genres of texts. Think of the situation in which someone has died—what sort of style and substance do we expect to hear in the text of the funeral eulogy (a situation that recurs for the living)? Think of the situation in which people are getting married—what sorts of style and substance are usually encountered in the texts of wedding sermons or the toasts during the receptions? Because people develop generic expectations for certain kinds of texts, a close reading can ask whether any given text is likely to be read by an audience with such expectations and, if so, whether the text meets or violates those expectations of style and substance. How a text meets or violates generic expectations has a lot to do with how it affects an audience.

We may also think of genre in a second sense, as a general category or type of text that is keyed to *narrative,* a concept we explored earlier in this chapter. A genre is *a recurring type of narrative.* Here, too, audience expectations are key. We all have a sense of the genres you might find on television: sports broadcasts, news programs, comedies, crime dramas, and so on. Similarly, we are all aware of the genres we find when we go to the movies. In fact, think of the previews or trailers that you see before a film as announcements of genre. They tell you what kind of narrative an upcoming movie will be. Think of how often you've decided to see or to avoid a film based on whether the preview signaled to you that the new release was of one genre or another ("A horror movie! Let's see that!" "Romantic comedy . . . maybe not.").

EXERCISE 3.6

❖ Break up into teams in your class. Each team's task is to find "previews" of future texts and identify ways in which previews announce textual genres. Two kinds of previews are easy. First, most movies have several previews before the actual feature begins. One team should go see a movie and pay close attention to how these previews tell viewers what sort of genre upcoming movies will belong to. Second, television is full of previews stuck in among the advertisements, telling you about future shows on that or related channels. How do we know what genres these upcoming shows are, based on those announcements? Think creatively about other kinds of "previews" we encounter that are actually announcements of genre; are there previews for upcoming political debates, sports events, or public festivities?

❖ When each team has taken careful notes of these previews, think about how previews very quickly and efficiently tell people the genre of future texts. How are these generic announcements made? What are the elements of these preview announcements that allow us to make judgments about genre?

❖ Compare your notes on how previews work with the theories of genre we've just discussed. How do previews raise expectations? How do they signal recurring contexts, substance, style, or kinds of narrative?

Let's put together the ideas of genre as based on audience expectations and as recurring types of narratives or recurring packages of substance, style, and context. Audiences usually have expectations for how certain genres work. Texts often call up one genre or another; they signal the audience to activate some of their expectations but not others. Sometimes contexts themselves call up a genre, as when the context is a funeral or a wedding. Once certain expectations are aroused, texts need to be read in terms of how they meet or violate those expectations. No general rule can be stated concerning what the rhetorical result will be when texts meet or violate generic expectations. Much depends on whether the person creating the text intended to follow or to violate genre, whether the audience will insist on genres being followed or violated, and what kind of violation occurs.

For example, the *Scary Movie* series of movies, which is quite popular, works by calling up audience expectations for the horror movie genre and then violating those expectations by creating satire and comedy. The close reader might inquire into the reasons for the films' popularity despite their generic violation. Does the comic breaking of the genre help the audience resolve the anxiety that is part of the horror genre? Is the horror genre not one "held sacred" by the audience such that its violation causes outrage? Are the films actually clear examples of another kind of genre? In comparison, one might think of the likely reaction were the president to go on television after some sort of national tragedy and deliver a comedy monologue when the audience expected a speech of a serious and somber genre. Why does one violation (*Scary Movie*) work but the other likely would not?

During 2006–2007, the insurance company GEICO ran a series of popular, humorous commercials featuring the outraged reactions of modern-day "cavemen" to fictitious commercials claiming that getting GEICO insurance is "so easy a caveman could do it." The television commercials were so popular that a comedy series was created out of them, which aired in the fall of 2007. There was nearly universal agreement that the television series was not very funny and did not live up to the expectations created by the commercials—it was canceled after only a few episodes. A close reader might think about audience expectations created by the genre of short television advertisements and whether those expectations can be met by half-hour comedy shows. Did the television series fail because it violated genre or simply because it did not live up to generic expectations (to be funny and amusing)?

The point in these examples is to ask the close critic to compare texts to the generic expectations raised by the texts or contexts. Reactions to texts can often be explained at least partially in terms of how the text met or violated those expectations. Let's turn now to the last technique of identifying form in texts, the idea of *persona*.

❖ PERSONA

A persona is *a role*, much like a character in a narrative, *that someone plays in connection to a text.* The word is from the Latin, meaning "to sound through," specifically to sound or speak through a mask that one wears in a play. A persona is therefore understood to be *an image one projects of who one is.* We might say of a public official we have met in casual circumstances, "Oh, she's not at all like her public persona." What we mean is that in the public texts the official creates, she is crafting a character, role, or image within that text.

It is useful to think of the idea of *persona* (or its plural, *personae*) in formal terms, as *a recurring kind of character or role that is taken up in connection with texts.* What sort of connection am I talking about? Here's where it gets complicated in some interesting ways. Several thinkers have written about this idea of persona. A closely related idea is that of *subject position,* explained by Brummett (*Rhetoric in Popular Culture,* 129–31), Althusser (85–126), and Hall (101–03). This theory holds that readers are asked by texts to take up a subject position in relationship to a text. A subject position is the kind of reader you have to become in order to make sense of the text. Subject positions are sometimes distinguished as *preferred, subversive,* or *inflected (negotiated).* One can take a *preferred* subject position, which is the one the text most clearly "appellates" or calls to in the reader. For instance, NFL football broadcasts clearly want you to be a fan of the game, and of course there are specific ways to do that: by becoming emotionally involved, by talking to the screen and to others in your presence, by sharing your football knowledge, and so forth. One can take a *subversive* subject position, in which one reads against the text, undermining the kind of reading stance the text calls for. Some people watch NFL football, perhaps unwillingly in the company of friends or a spouse who is a fan, subversively. They fight the call to be a fan all the way. They may yawn openly, read a magazine, or ridicule the commentary. One can also take a variety of *inflected* or *negotiated* subject positions that fall between the preferred or the oppositional. Someone from Mexico might watch NFL football with interest but constantly compare it to soccer. Another person might be a fan but not of the particular teams playing and so may make disparaging comments about the game compared to the favored team's play. A subject position is our response to the ways that texts call us to take on certain roles so as to read the text.

There is certainly political and social impact in whether one takes preferred, subversive, or inflected subject positions. When we take a preferred position, we go along with the broadest and most popular social expectations of whom to be. In contrast, Rachel Rubin and Jeffrey Melnick report that in the turbulent 1930s, when many Americans were out of work and feeling not so inclined to support the status quo, many audiences of gangster movies cheered for the bad guys (the gangsters) and booed the authorities (17–48). Negotiated positions can likewise involve finding a political stance for oneself somewhere between saying yes and saying no.

Here, I'd like to follow the terminology and logic of a persona as a role someone plays in connection to a text. The works of James Arnt Aune and Edwin Black suggest three personae that come into being every time a text is read. A text suggests a *first persona,* which is the role, image, or character of the one who created the text, the person or entity speaking to you through the text. This is an interesting concept, given the fact that many or most texts we encounter today are produced by quite a few people rather than only one. Nevertheless, a text will project an image or role that something or someone might take in order to produce the text. Texts vary in the distinctiveness of their first personae. Most of us would likely recognize instantly a poem by Dr. Seuss, even if we had never read it before, because he has such a distinctive voice and persona. Gangsta rap tends to portray strong first personae, a very clear sense of the speaker.

A text also suggests or calls for a *second persona,* which is the audience or the person reading the text. This concept tells us that texts call us to take on certain roles or to be certain kinds of people if we want to engage the particular text. Texts speak to some roles but not others. If you have ever felt that a text—a book, a lecture, a television advertisement—"talked down" to you, the text likely implied a second persona that you did not like and did not want to accept. If you send an e-mail of complaint to a company, think about how your phrasing of the e-mail makes a statement about the person on the receiving end.

Finally, texts suggest a *third persona,* a sense of the Other, a stance or role allotted to "those people over there" in relationship to the text and to the first and second personae. People attending a political caucus or convention often make clear constructions of a third persona, an Other, belonging to a rival party. People gossiping about a person not present do the same. To understand these concepts more clearly, let's do a short exercise.

EXERCISE 3.7

❖ Individually or in teams, record one-hour news broadcasts from several television news shows or channels, preferably at the same time (so you can compare the stories reported). You might record the major broadcast or cable networks, like ABC, CBS, NBC, PBS, Fox, CNN, MSNBC, and others.

❖ Now, systematically study the first, second, and third personae created by each interaction between text and reader. For instance, who does CNN say they are, and how does that differ from who the Financial News Network says they are (first persona)? Who do the major networks of ABC, CBS, and NBC say that you are, in comparison to the implied reader of public television news broadcasts (second persona)? Do any of the broadcasts have a strong sense of who a third party is, some other group or entity who is not you and not the broadcaster (third persona)? You might especially find third personae suggested by Lou Dobbs on CNN or by Bill O'Reilly on Fox.

(Continued)

(Continued)

❖ Think about the creation of first, second, and third personae as an important part of the work of each text. Ask yourself what the long-term effect would be in terms of how people thought of themselves, of news organizations, and of other people and groups if people regularly followed one network or another for the news.

I want to stress that these personae created by texts are *formal.* There are recurring patterns or types of personae, and these standard categories are called to as texts tell us who they, we, and those folks over there are. Just as there is a wide but limited range of forms that texts can follow, so is there a wide but limited range of personae that you, I, creators of texts, and others may take on. In fact, personae must be formal for us to recognize them when we encounter them in close reading, because forms are familiar and recurring. If a text (say, a college lecture) calls you (second persona) to be a serious, contemplative scholar, it is calling you to step into the pattern of a reading role. We have seen the persona of the serious, contemplative scholar played out in movies, on television, and in person as we observe our fellow A students or listen to our learned professors. So we have *expectations* (that term again) of how to be the serious, contemplative scholar. Texts call people to recognizable reading roles in the expectation that people will recognize the call and step into the role.

Texts also express recurring forms of personae to tell you who "the authors" are (first persona). If you are called by a professor's lecture to be a serious, contemplative scholar, the professor is likely to be enacting a formal role as well. If you've taken several classes, you can likely identify some patterns of "professorial" roles: the highly structured, high-toned lecturer; the sit-cross-legged-on-a-table discussant; the teacher who runs around the room as if his clothing were burning. And then there are recurring forms of personae attributed to Others (third persona) by texts. There are formal ways *not* to be the serious, contemplative scholar, and when the professor reminds you to keep up with the reading, to use reputable sources in your citations, to carefully research your topics, he or she may be implying your difference from other forms of personae (the slackard, the plagiarist) you may have observed in others.

EXERCISE 3.8

❖ Collect some newspapers or weeklies that are widely read. A good selection might be *USA Today*, the *New York Times*, your local city newspaper, and the *National Enquirer*. Read three or four issues of each so you can detect the patterns emerging in each one.

❖ Now, identify the formal, patterned personae that each publication implies. Who does the *Times* say it is? Who does the *Enquirer* say you are? Who does your local paper imply that residents of other cities or states are?

As with genre, the personae that a text creates may depart from expectations. The personae may be disturbing or challenging departures from recurring, formal patterns. But as with genre, we must understand deviations from form and expectations in terms of those forms. Think of a song that called forth unexpected personae or crossed formal lines in some unexpected ways. For example, the rapper Mase developed a "bad boy" persona in his debut album *Harlem World*. Shortly thereafter, he found religion. His next album, *Welcome Back*, might be read as calling forth some personae that were not quite true to previous form. He mixes his previous "bad boy" persona with a "nice" one. Think about how his audience, trained to take on a second persona that can appreciate the "gangsta" first persona of *Harlem World*, might negotiate the new call for personae in *Welcome Back*. Or think of the whole musical career of Will Smith, who has enacted a first persona that has been an interesting and sometimes unstable mix of the nice family guy and television comedy star persona *with* a harder, more driving (if not yet gangsta) rapper image; that has called forth a similarly complex second persona among his fans; and that has implied a critical third persona for his competitors and those who criticize his "niceness."

❖ FORM AND POLITICS

Let me call your attention to the relevance of narrative, genre, and persona to the management of social and political issues. These elements of form can carry important effects that manage power distribution. President Barack Obama was widely admired for running a nearly flawless campaign in 2008. "Flawless" can be well explained in terms of cohesion and sequence: Obama and his aides were almost always on message, almost always stressing the same "story." Many political candidates wanted to be seen as the underdog during the campaign, since we are used to patterns of tension and resolution in which the underdog wins at the end. Several observers have suggested that the genre of a story in which an African American family moves into the White House was created decades ago in narratives such as *The Cosby Show*. Looking at film, *New York Times* critics Manohla Dargis and A. O. Scott argued that "evolving cinematic roles have prepared America to have a Black man in charge," and they cite such films as *I Am Legend* and *Guess Who's Coming to Dinner*. President Obama and his family are not the Huxtables, but a pattern was laid down in American consciousness that may have contributed to their acceptance. Some political observers have argued that enduring sexism in U.S. society prevented the American people from seeing a woman like Senator Hillary Rodham Clinton in the role of president. The implication is that leadership roles can be gendered, and the public tends to want its leaders to enact recognizably male personae.

Outright discrimination and social persecution have become unfashionable, but politics may still be waged through form. The film *Brokeback Mountain* featured a loving, if conflicted, relationship between two cowboys (played by straight actors), yet the form of the story led the characters to their doom. A gay relationship is not condemned in terms of content but is shown to be hopeless. What sort of political and social effects might that pattern have?

❖ SUMMARY AND LOOKING AHEAD

In this chapter we have looked at techniques for detecting and using form in close reading. We learned that *form is the structure, the pattern, that organizes a text*. Also, we discovered that detection of form is important because *form moves people more than content does*. Form in a text helps people grasp information, and it is rhetorically powerful. This can be observed through our everyday use of mnemonic devices, which are highly formal ways to make content or information accessible to us: *A mnemonic device is a trick you use to help you memorize something*.

The groups of techniques we learned for seeing form in texts are *narrative, genre*, and *persona*. Narrative is, of course, the storylike form of a text, and we learned that *most, if not all, texts contain storylike forms or narratives to some extent*. Three elements of narrative are found in texts: *coherence and sequence, tension and resolution*, and *alignment and opposition*.

Next, we studied form in genre. You learned that genre is *a recurring type of text within a context.* As such, a genre has recurring *situational* and *stylistic* responses to recurring kinds of *contexts.* One can also think of a genre as *a recurring type of narrative.* You learned that the previews we see of coming attractions, shown before feature films, function largely by signaling to us which genre these new movies will belong to.

Finally, we studied techniques for identifying *personae* in texts. A persona is *a role,* much like a character in a narrative, *that someone plays in connection to a text.* Persona is related to the concept of *subject position.* We studied three kinds of subject positions: *preferred, subversive,* and *inflected (negotiated).* You learned that the experience of reading a text generates a *first persona* (a role or character that the person or entity behind the text takes on), a *second persona* (a role the audience or reader is asked to take on), and a *third persona* (attributions of a role to some other person or group). You learned that, like genres, personae are highly formal. Finally, you learned that form and narrative can carry social and political impact, even beyond content.

In the next chapter, I explain some techniques for seeing *transformations* in close readings. Often, some part of a text will support meanings that go well beyond the literal meaning of what is said or shown. How to see beyond the surface of a text to what lies beneath is the purpose of our next set of techniques.

4

Transformations in Texts

Seeing beneath the Surface

❖ ❖ ❖

Y ou have probably looked at clouds and thought about what else they resemble: bears, elephants, ships, and so forth. With a little imagination you can see "real" castles in the sky. Texts are somewhat like clouds in that way. Every now and then, we come across a word, a phrase, a nonverbal sign that seems to resemble or mean something other than what it appears to be literally. Look at Figure 4.1, for instance. You are looking at a bottle that has been visually altered to resemble a woman. Understanding the appeal of the ad depends on understanding how that alteration works, how the image is both a woman and a bottle at the same time. Understanding how you can see one thing while also seeing another, as you do when you look at clouds, is an important technique of close reading. In texts, signs are often more than or other than what they seem to be.

These elements of texts in which one thing seems to be another are *transformations,* in the sense that a given cloud might look like a train that has been transformed into water vapor and set in the sky. A widely repeated joke before the election of President Obama—or is it a joke?— is that Bill Clinton was "the first Black president." Such a statement treats President Clinton as a kind of transformation, as an African

To view this image in full resolution, please visit www.sagepub.com/brummettstudy.

American in disguise, if you will. The claim also implicitly argues that to understand President Clinton, we must see him as if he came from that particular cultural background. A close reader of the text that is President Clinton, or of texts about the president, will need to take that transformation into account.

The king of transformations in recent Western culture is Sigmund Freud, the nineteenth- and twentieth-century Austrian psychoanalyst who developed a system for interpreting the meaning of signs in our mental lives. He applied this system particularly to the interpretation of dreams. If you dream about a house, for example, Freud would argue that the house is a transformation of yourself—you are dreaming about yourself. Thus, if you dream that you discover some new, unexpected rooms in your house, you are actually dreaming that there are dimensions of yourself yet to be discovered. You really are dreaming about a house but also about yourself. To understand what the text of your dream means, we must understand its transformations. Freud has encouraged generations of close readers to think about how transformations might run throughout texts.

This chapter teaches you how to look for some common transformations in texts. You will find that looking for transformations is a technique that cuts across many different methods of close reading and that transformations are explained by several theories that deal with how and why the transformations work rhetorically. In this chapter, I focus on four kinds of transformations as explained by Kenneth Burke, the great rhetorical theorist to whom I have referred earlier.

A transformation is a *turning* of a word or image. In Figure 4.1, you know to "turn" the image of the bottle, to tell yourself not to take the picture literally but to use visual cues in the picture (the "flip hairstyle" of the red wax) so as to begin to see a woman where the bottle is. *Trope* is a word derived from the Greek *tropos*, which means "turning." We find it in the words *phototropic*, or "turning toward light," and *heliotropic*, or "turning toward the sun," terms that describe what plants do. *A trope is a category of textual devices in which the literal, ordinary meaning of a sign or image must be turned or altered to arrive at what the sign or image means in a text.* Through the history of studying texts, writers have identified quite a number of these tropes. In his book *A Grammar of Motives*, Burke argues that there are four master tropes. These four tropes, or forms of turning and transformation, are *metaphor, metonymy, synecdoche, and irony* (503–18). It is likely that some of those terms are familiar to you and others not, but I will explain them all in detail shortly.

Burke previews his discussion of the four master tropes in this useful summation:

"For *metaphor* we could substitute *perspective*; For *metonymy* we could substitute *reduction*; For *synecdoche* we could substitute *representation*; For *irony* we could substitute *dialectic*" (*Grammar*, 503). Burke's definition of each trope tells us what it means that we find one trope or another in a text. His scheme tells us of the mental and emotional roles played by each one. When we use metaphor, we take a perspective on a subject, and so the close reader of a text can see the presence of metaphor as a particular way of seeing a subject matter. If a text wants to reduce, simplify, or downscale its subject, it turns to metonymy. Representation of a subject is accomplished through synecdoche; the subject is re-presented to an audience. And irony sets up the back-and-forth mental discussion of dialectic, in which the bonds created by conversational exchange are established.

As with so many of Burke's charts and schemes, the four categories here are not meant to be kept sharply distinct. A transformation in a text may well seem to be based on more than one kind of trope. As the close reader begins examining one kind of trope as a technique, he or she may edge toward identifying the other three as the reading progresses. Any given sign or expression in a text may well seem to be more than one trope at the same time.

In this chapter I explain techniques of looking in texts for metaphor, metonymy, synecdoche, and irony that encourage a creative shifting of focus from one trope to another. The idea is to enable you to see how transformations work, not to follow some rigid structure. Let me now begin by explaining the first of the master tropes, metaphor.

❖ METAPHOR

Burke offers this explanation of *metaphor*: "Metaphor is a device for seeing something in terms of something else. It brings out the thisness of a that, or the thatness of a this" (*Grammar*, 503). You will recall from his summary, quoted earlier, that Burke sees the essence of metaphor as *perspective*. We use metaphor when we want to see something not as it is or for what it is but from the perspective of something else. *Parables* in the Bible or other sacred texts work as metaphors in this way. When St. Luke relates the parable of the Prodigal Son (Luke 15:11–32), it is a metaphor, and for that reason a perspective, on the subject of forgiveness. It says, Think about forgiveness as if a father gave an irresponsible son great wealth, and so forth.

Metaphors are common, and examples abound. Consider this: "The center on their team is a real tank." Notice that to make sense of that statement, you must "turn" the meaning of the words; the expression is a trope. Unless you think the speaker is crazy, you know that he or she does not really mean to say that the center on their team is literally a military vehicle that rolls around on tracks. Instead, you know that the speaker has turned the literal meaning of the statement and wants you to think of their center as having tanklike characteristics. To paraphrase Burke in the preceding paragraph, the speaker wants to bring out the "tankness" of the center. The speaker is using the tank to take a *perspective* on the center.

The first cousin of metaphor is *simile*. A simile is to say that one thing is *like* or *as* another thing. In that sense, a simile is an attenuated or diluted metaphor. Some examples are "She's as sharp as a tack," "Joel can run like the wind," "You are as slow as molasses." I'm sure you can think of many ordinary metaphors and similes beyond these. Often, favorite expressions of friends and family members take the form of metaphors and similes. Perhaps your older relatives would say, "easy as pie" or "He's a pistol!"

Metaphors are quite familiar to all of us, and we use them constantly. They are a major tool of expression. In fact, I used a metaphor in that last sentence! To refer to a form of language—metaphor—as a tool is a kind of turning of language. We think of tools as hardware that we use to create, build, or repair things. To refer to metaphors as tools is to turn the usual meaning of words so as to see them as though they were tools, hammers and chisels and so forth. Metaphors and similes are essential parts of everyday speech.

An important technique of close reading is to look for metaphors. Because they are so widely used, we may not notice when a speaker or author creates this particular trope. Why is it important to look for metaphors? Metaphors urge people to take a perspective on certain actions, objects, and events, and they do this in two ways: Metaphors should be studied for their *implications* and for their *extensions*.

When we turn the literal meaning of an action, object, or event by making it a metaphor, that thing picks up some of the meanings of the other action, object, or event with which it is paired. A useful distinction is made between those two parts of the metaphor. The action, object, or event you are talking about—what the writer wants the reader to see differently—is called the *tenor* of the metaphor. The tenor is what the writer wants to create a perspective on. The other action, object, or event with which it is paired is called the *vehicle* of the metaphor. When we say, "This political campaign is a train wreck," we want the listener to learn something about the political campaign, which is the tenor of that metaphor. We don't care so much whether the listener learns about train wrecks. Here, the train wreck is the vehicle of the metaphor; it is what we use to get some perspective on the political campaign.

Any action, object, or event can be either tenor or vehicle. We may move from saying, "This political campaign is a train wreck" to saying, "Sadly, that train wreck was as predictable as the rising sun." Now, we are talking about a train wreck as tenor and using the vehicle of the rising sun (and its certainty each morning) as the vehicle to help us see something about the train wreck.

When I refer to *implications*, I am calling attention to the parallels or comparisons urged upon the audience by a metaphor. When I say,

"Your visit is a real gift to me," I want you to take note of what is implied by my equating your visit and a gift. I don't spell the implications out—if I did, my expression would become an analogy or a comparison, not a metaphor. The metaphor depends on your teasing out the implications. Metaphors usually depend on the speaker or writer making a pretty good guess which implications will be teased out. I say, "Your visit is a real gift to me" in full confidence that you will find no implications in my utterance that will cause you to take offense but instead will be pleased.

But suppose I'm wrong? When we use a given vehicle to help us understand the tenor, we always run the risk that certain *unplanned implications* will be transferred from the vehicle to the tenor. The speaker or writer may be unaware of these—even the audience may be unaware—but meanings can creep into our thinking nevertheless, through implications. These are worth exploring in close reading.

If we say, in our earlier example, "The center on their team is a tank," surely we want to imply that their center is big, tough, and dangerous. Is there any danger that people will also pick up the implication that their center is inhuman? That their center can feel no pain? That their center is a true enemy who needs to be destroyed physically? Likely not, but the close reader may want to look into these possibilities. Close readers should always think about a wide range of possible implications of metaphor. One way to do that is to look for other signs elsewhere in the text that support these more sinister implications of "tank." If we find more literal or figurative expressions of their center's inhumanity and physical dangerousness in the same text, that is a clue to the direction the implications of the metaphor are taking. But if, as expected, most of the text has signs that stress the center's physical prowess and athletic ability, we may feel confident in ruling out the implication of dangerousness.

In Chapter 1 I explained the importance of historical and textual context in close reading. Both kinds of context are important in helping us to understand the implications of a metaphor. "She came to us as a drenching rain" means very different things, depending on whether one is speaking in the context of a long drought (she is welcome) or of a recent days-long hurricane (she is really not what we need right now). Different meanings are implied for the tenor (she) by that vehicle (rain) in different contexts. Context may also be created within the text, as it would be were you reading a short story about a drought or a hurricane. How we read the implications of metaphors is thus determined by context.

In Chapter 1 I also explained the importance of considering how different audiences may read a text. If a political commentator calls the president a cowboy—and if it's clear that this is a trope, the president not being a literal cowboy—it would make a difference whether you were reading that metaphor in rural Wyoming or in downtown New York City. The metaphor may be a compliment in Wyoming but not so flattering in New York. In our earlier example, calling the center on another team a tank might be read differently by a war veteran than by someone who had never served in the military. Audience perspective brings some implications to the forefront of awareness while deemphasizing others. Let's get a little experience in working out the implications of metaphors.

EXERCISE 4.1

❖ First we will work with Figure 4.2. This is a visual metaphor or simile, isn't it? Try to express it in words: "The Macallan drinker is a butterfly" or something to that effect. Think about the ways in which the creator of the ad has turned literal meaning, and the reader must realize that to make the text work.

Figure 4.2

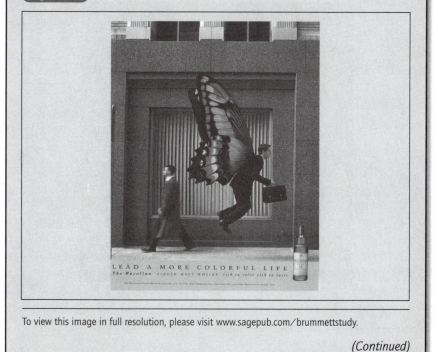

LEAD A MORE COLORFUL LIFE
The Macallan SINGLE MALT WHISKY rich in color rich in taste

To view this image in full resolution, please visit www.sagepub.com/brummettstudy.

(Continued)

(Continued)

❖ On your own or in groups, tease out some of the implications of the visual metaphor in Figure 4.2. Butterflies are beautiful, light, free . . . are those implications likely to be intended by the creator of the text? However, butterflies also live only a short while! Are most readers likely to find that implication in the metaphor? Does the rest of the text help us decide which implications come to the fore? Does the butterfly metaphor create implications of gender, class, race, and so forth? For instance, would most people attribute stereotypical male or female meanings to butterflies? When might readers find those gender implications in the metaphor of the ad?

❖ Examine Figure 4.3. Clearly this is a metaphor, a turning of the literal. Think for a moment about what you are looking at. The sponsor of the text wants to sell ceramic tile, so we may suppose that tile is the tenor of the metaphor. What is its vehicle?

Figure 4.3

To view this image in full resolution, please visit www.sagepub.com/brummettstudy.

❖ What implications are suggested by this particular metaphor in Figure 4.3? The object into which the tiles have been "turned" is feminine rather than masculine, correct? Is that implication desired by the creator of the text, do you think? Will most readers of the text find that implication?

❖ For a third part of this exercise, go to an online search engine and type in these words: cancer body politic. Quite a range of political commentaries will come up. Read some of them. Most of them will assert that such-and-such a prominent person or political party or way of thinking is a "cancer" on the body of American (at least) politics.

❖ What are the implications of using *cancer* as a vehicle in a metaphor? Think about whether cancer is something you "catch" from someone else— another person, another country—or whether it is in some sense a failure of the self, of the body. Evaluate the implications of cancer as a vehicle, and think about when it is warranted and when it is not.

Metaphors also have *extension*. A metaphor is extended when quite a few parallels between tenor and vehicle are asserted. Often an extension is done systematically: a base metaphor is created, and then ways in which the vehicle allows a perspective on the tenor are explained by the text. Figure 4.4 is an example of a briefly extended metaphor. The tenor that is the automobile is turned—what is it turned into? An aircraft interior, of course. Notice how the description on the left side of the text extends that metaphor. The description doesn't just assert the parallel between car and airplane—it extends it, finding several parallels. Given the need for economy of space and brevity in a magazine ad, this is an impressive degree of extension.

You can think of an extended metaphor as a metaphor in which *implications* are repeatedly emphasized, discovered and rediscovered, and carried forward into new applications. Figure 4.4 asks you to consider several implications in one metaphor. Metaphors that are good candidates for extension must therefore have good potential for developing these implications at length. There must be a lot of potential for linking tenor and vehicle in fruitful ways. The skillful development of implications can extend a metaphor throughout a whole text.

Extensions of metaphors can stretch across a variety of texts. In fact, an extended metaphor can underlie whole philosophies, political programs, even religions. For example, in the congressional elections of 1994, the Republican Party, seeking to gain control of Congress from

Figure 4.4

To view this image in full resolution, please visit www.sagepub.com/brummettstudy.

the Democratic Party, called its party platform the Contract with America. The metaphor of a contract was extended throughout the campaign and even after the resulting Republican victory. A contract creates moral and ethical obligations. A contract is a kind of promise; people demand accountability for contracts, and parties to a contract will often report on what they have done to fulfill the contract. Even after the election, the Republican Party used the contract metaphor to describe their legislative program with great success—the party would hold power in both houses of Congress until the elections of 2006. Let's further explore the idea of an extended metaphor through what may become an extended exercise.

EXERCISE 4.2

❖ This will require some hard work on your part, individually or in teams. Find a stable group in the community whose texts are accessible to you in one way or another. You might start collecting media coverage about a sports team at your school. If you work for a company that puts out memos, flyers, e-mails, Web pages, and so forth, you might collect some of them. You might be part of a local religious community and begin gathering the texts it puts out in the form of bulletins, newsletters, doctrinal statements, and the like. What you want is a group or organization that has lasted over time and that talks about itself or is talked about in ways that create lots of texts.

❖   Now, read the texts you have gathered closely to consider whether an extended metaphor consistently underlies those texts. You won't always find an extended metaphor in this way, but they organize many texts for such groups more often than you might think. One way to think about this task is to ask whether a sports team, for instance, is repeatedly described as if it were a family. If so, that would be an extended metaphor. Track the ways in which the implications of the sports team-as-family metaphor are extended across different texts and times. Other possibilities might be that the team is described as a business or a military unit. Evaluate the rhetorical impact of the extended metaphor that is used to talk about the group you are studying.

We have seen ways to look for metaphors in close reading. We have been mindful to note the ways that metaphors create perspectives on their subject. Now, let us turn to the second of the tropes we are considering: *metonymy.*

❖   METONYMY

Burke describes *metonymy* in this way: "The basic 'strategy' in metonymy is this: to convey some incorporeal or intangible state in terms of the corporeal or tangible" (*Grammar,* 506). *Metonymy expresses an abstract idea in terms of something physical or material.* You may recall that earlier in this chapter I quoted Burke as saying that metonymy is a kind of *reduction,* and so it is. An abstract, general, hard-to-pin-down idea is expressed in something concrete, specific, and tangible. An idea is *reduced* to an action, object, or event. The cognitive and emotional move in metonymy, then, is to go to the concrete, to translate abstractions and grand concepts into the hard and fast.

I noted earlier that some proverbs and old sayings are metaphors. Others are metonymies. The abstract value of thrift is expressed in the proverb "A penny saved is a penny earned." The abstract value of timeliness and thinking ahead are metonymized in the more concrete sewing reference "A stitch in time saves nine." We might see some of the appeal of metonymy here: the focus on homely and homespun examples that relate to everyday experiences, in place of abstract or "preachy" principles.

Political campaign season is often a good place to see metonymy in widespread use. In the American presidential campaign of 2007–2008, candidates of both the Republican and Democratic parties presented themselves as the very embodiment of abstract ideas: hope, patriotism, conservative values, experience, good judgment, and so forth. It is not at all unusual for a political candidate to describe him- or herself as (fill in this space with an abstract virtue)-in-the-flesh. "I am the education candidate," one might say, while another might claim to be the embodiment of "national security." These are abstract ideas: hope, security, education, and so forth. The actual physical candidate is not abstract but is a metonymy of those abstractions.

Politicians are also fond of complaining about Washington (or the name of the state capital). What they mean to complain about is big government, arrogance, wasteful policies, entrenched bureaucracy, and so forth, all of which are so widespread that they are hard to pin down. Therefore, big government, arrogance, wasteful policies, and the like are rather abstract. We metonymize those abstractions when we refer to Washington, which is an actual, concrete city, this way.

Where I live, in the great state of Texas, political candidates complain about Austin when they want to complain about the abstract sins of government. Austin also serves as a second kind of metonymy within the state, for it is a by-and-large liberal city within a by-and-large conservative state, so if someone wants to complain about liberal ideas, they will sometimes metonymize those abstractions by complaining about Austin. Of course, those who actually live in Austin often metonymize it as a city of culture, sophistication, and tolerance.

Metonymy in politics is very ancient. We see it in the old practice, now discarded, of referring to a king or queen as the entire country, as if they were the entire country. The abstract idea of a whole country is thus reduced to the monarch. A long time ago, people would sometimes refer to the king of France as simply France. It is reported that at the coronation of England's Queen Elizabeth II in 1952, the king of Norway, a friendly, humble, and affable fellow, went around shaking the hands of his fellow monarchs, saying, "You don't remember me; I'm Norway" (Lambert).

We find metonymy in all sorts of texts, from this morning's news blog to great literature. Consider this well-known poem by the American poet William Carlos Williams:

> *so much depends*
> *upon*
>   *a red wheel*
> *barrow*
>   *glazed with rain*
> *water*
>   *beside the white*
> *chickens*

Williams was part of what is referred to as the imagist school of poetry, and the motto of that group was "no ideas but in things." You might say that the imagists were therefore a thoroughly metonymic group of poets. Ideas, which are always abstract, were to be expressed in things, which are always concrete reductions. In Williams's poem, the abstract idea is not expressed, only the metonymic reduction. That is the point of reading the poem, to tease out the idea being reduced to this one clear image. The poem even helps us along in thinking about broader ideas implied by the reduction, because "so much depends upon" the few concrete objects that follow. What, we are led to ask, is it that matters so much? How might you answer that question about the poem? In answering, you will be interpreting a metonymy.

Looking for metonymy is a useful technique in close reading because it helps us to see when a named action, object, or event stands for an abstract principle or idea. The reader can detect metonymies in two ways, or in two different directions, so to speak. First, the reader can be on the lookout for actions, objects, and events that seem to carry an extra-heavy weight of meaning, when they seem to imply a great deal more than just what they are materially. This technique "starts small" and begins with attention to concrete references in texts. You might notice that the image of a pistol plays a central part in a music video, for instance. Is it standing in for some more abstract idea?

A second way to use metonymy in close reading is to "start large." After a first round of reading a text, you might have a general impression that it is about some big ideas in some way. Ask yourself which concrete actions, objects, or events depicted in the text are metonymies of those big ideas. Let's do some work in studying metonymy in actual texts.

EXERCISE 4.3

❖ Read Cormac McCarthy's Pulitzer Prize-winning novel *The Road*. If you don't have time for the whole thing, five pages will give you the idea. This may be the bleakest, most powerful book you have ever read. It depicts a father and son struggling along a road in a devastated post-apocalyptic landscape where the sun is constantly hidden from view by blankets of cloud, ash, and rain. Nothing grows, the seas are dead, and the people who survive do it by scavenging for the few remaining sources of food and water they can find. The whole book is written at the level of specific, concrete actions, objects, and events. There is a gun with a specific number of cartridges left in it; there is a field of mummified apples; there is a storm shelter full of canned goods; there are grocery store carts; there is the road, and so forth. Yet it is clear that these wretched actions, objects, and events must stand for big, powerful, more abstract ideas because the novel as a whole is so terribly moving. Treat *The Road* as a museum of metonymies, and work on what is metonymized and how.

❖ Identify a current human-interest news story. Perhaps there is a political scandal going on. Perhaps a child has fallen down a well in a distant state. Perhaps a celebrity has behaved badly. In most of these cases, nobody really needs to know the particular story; we don't need to know about the celebrity being rushed to the detox center or the politician caught with his pants down. Yet the public seems fascinated by such stories. Treat them as metonymies, and use evidence from the texts of these stories to identify the abstract ideas that are being expressed in these particular actions, objects, and events.

I noted earlier that these four tropes we are studying will merge into each other. It is not hard to find examples of tropes that seem to be hybrids, performing more than one task. For instance, here is a well-known poem by the American poet Emily Dickinson:

Hope is the thing with feathers
That perches in the soul,
And sings the tune—without the words,
And never stops at all,

And sweetest in the gale is heard;
And sore must be the storm
That could abash the little bird
That kept so many warm.

I've heard it in the chillest land,
And on the strangest sea;
Yet, never, in extremity,
It asked a crumb of me.

Clearly there is some sort of trope here, for the literal meaning of a bird is being turned somehow. I believe the poem is perched (pun intended) between metaphor, the first trope we studied, and metonymy. Clearly there is the metaphor "Hope is a bird." But notice how hope is also an abstract idea that is embodied in the concrete object, a bird. The close reader need not decide once and for all whether part of a text is this or that trope. What is useful in close reading is to note the complicated tropes through which texts create meanings, often in ways that go beyond the ability of our classificatory schemes and techniques to name. Think about how Dickinson's poem creates *both* the perspective that Burke ascribes to metaphor *and* the reduction that he says is key to metonymy. Notice that thinking about both perspective and reduction helps you to understand what the poem means. We may expect to find similar overlap with the third trope we now turn to, synecdoche.

❖   SYNECDOCHE

Burke says of *synecdoche*, "For this purpose we consider synecdoche in the usual range of dictionary sense, with such meanings as: part for the whole, whole for the part, container for the contained, sign for the thing signified, material for the thing made, . . . cause for effect, effect for cause, genus for species, species for genus, etc. All such conversions imply an integral relationship, a relationship of convertibility, between the two terms" (*Grammar,* 508). As I noted earlier, synecdoche is the trope of *representation.* Let's see how representation is implied in some of the synecdochic characteristics Burke mentions.

Sometimes we refer to part of something when we mean the whole thing. In doing so we pick the part that represents what we want to emphasize about the whole thing. A ship captain might call, "All hands on deck," or a farmer might go out to employ some "hired hands." The captain wants more than just hands to come flopping up out of the hold and onto the deck, and the farmer wants more than just hands to go bring in the harvest. But we say "hands" because that part of the whole sailor or the whole agricultural worker represents the "handiness," the ability to do skilled work, that we want to emphasize about the whole sailor or worker. If we are annoyed with someone, we might call, "Get your butt in here!" We want the entire person to come, but we refer to a particularly undignified part of that whole because we want to say something unpleasant about the person at the moment.

We can also refer to the whole of something when we mean a part. Agencies that collect blood donations sometimes call for the public to "give the gift of life." Of course, if you go to donate blood, they won't actually take your life! They take your blood, which is only part of life, but they call blood (a part) by the whole (life) to emphasize how important blood is to staying alive.

Business executives are sometimes referred to as "suits," as when a factory line worker says of a mechanical failure, "Well, the suits won't like this." Uniformed police officers are sometimes referred to as "uniforms," as when plainclothes detectives might put in a call to headquarters to "send some uniforms down here to quiet the crowd." Both of these are synecdoches using Burke's "container for the contained." The words are for clothing that "contains" the executive or the officer within. The suit is taken to represent the formality of the executive; the uniform is taken to represent the visible show of force that is the actual officer.

A country-western tune might refer to "the ring on her finger," which is a sign, when what is meant is a person's marital status, the thing signified by the ring. When we refer to clothing as "threads" or "rags," we are using synecdoche—that is, as Burke says, referring to "material for the thing made." As you can see above, the list that Burke gives is a long one, but the idea of representation runs through each example.

As with all of our master tropes, synecdoche may be found in many real social and political settings. At this writing, Nicolas Sarkozy, the president of France, has generated much controversy over his plan to require French schoolchildren to learn the life story of a deceased World War II Holocaust victim (Sciolino). Each French child today would receive a brief history of a specific child who died in the concentration camps seventy or eighty years ago at about the age of today's French child. Clearly this is an example of synecdoche. The deceased Holocaust child is to represent all Holocaust victims. In fact, it is the specific representation of all of those victims in each particular dead child's story that makes the suggestion so poignant. The issue continues to be debated, with sharp disagreement on both sides.

Synecdoche works in texts because what the speaker or writer refers to is especially able to represent what the speaker or writer wants to say about that which is represented. If I refer to your small dog as an "ankle biter," I am using the low height and relatively minor potential harm of a bitten ankle to represent what is inconsequential, small, and annoying about your dog (part for whole). If I refer to all the (fill in name of expensive car here) that pulled up to the premier of a new film, I am using the expense and quality of the car to say something about the glitz and glamor of those inside the cars (container for the thing contained). The close reader should pay attention to what is stressed or featured by the main action, object, or event under examination in a synecdoche.

The four tropes we are reviewing are both distinct and overlapping. Synecdoche differs from metaphor in that it retains some literal truth: there is a real connection between the sailor and the hand, between blood and life. Metaphors pair together two things which are not in fact connected. Synecdoche differs from metonymy in that metonymy is always the reduction of an abstract idea to something concrete. Synecdoche is not always interested in representing that which is abstract, although it might sometimes. But as we saw in comparing metonymy and metaphor above, we can think of borderline cases in which a given trope may seem to be of more than one kind. In the previous example of the wedding ring representing marriage, there is a healthy amount of metonymy mixed into that synecdoche, since marriage can be thought of as a somewhat abstract concept. Let's do an exercise that will help us to see synecdoche at work.

EXERCISE 4.4

❖   Identify a public figure currently in the news. It may be a politician, it may be a celebrity. Pay particular attention to what is said in the news about everyday actions, objects, and events connected to this public figure. Perhaps there will be frequent reports of what the candidate eats, for instance. Perhaps the clothing of a candidate will be mentioned often.

❖   Work on how these references to everyday actions, objects, and events represent the public figure. Is a politician represented differently depending on whether he or she is reported as eating fried-chicken dinners at the county fair with voters or described as sipping white wine and nibbling on Camembert cheese at a black-tie gala? You might also notice consistent patterns of representation and the rhetorical work they do. For instance, female politicians tend to draw much more commentary about what they wear than do male politicians.

Now we turn to the last of our four master tropes, *irony*.

❖ IRONY

Of the four master tropes, irony is the only one for which Burke does not provide a succinct definition. This is likely because it is both one of the most common and one of the least understood of the tropes. A single definition is hard to pin down.

It is sometimes said that we live in an age of irony. Irony in this sense may be found, for example, all throughout *The Daily Show with Jon Stewart*. Suppose you hear a political candidate give a terribly long speech, one that rambles on and on without end. Afterward you might turn to a friend sitting next to you, roll your eyes, and say, "Well, *that* was short and to the point, wasn't it?" You are being ironic. You are counting on your friend to turn the literal meaning of your expression, to read it as exactly the opposite of what your words actually mean. Furthermore, if irony works, your friend will know that you know that the friend is intended to turn the meaning. Irony in this sense depends on this little dance that the two of you will do together. That kind of back-and-forth understanding is what Burke means by equating irony with dialectic. Irony in a text creates a dialogue or conversation between author and reader.

When people claim that we are in an age of irony, they are saying that a great deal of public discourse is ironic, is meant to be turned, as is *The Daily Show*. The satirical newspaper *The Onion* is completely ironic from start to finish. Another example of a highly ironic popular text would be the comedy routine of "Larry the Cable Guy," who is part of the *Blue Collar Comedy Tour* seen on several television channels. We are often invited to laugh at the character of Larry, but it is clear that the comedian intends you to do so, that he is not as clueless as the character, and therefore a bond is created between the comedian and the audience. You might think of examples of the prevalence of irony in other television shows, movies, and so forth.

Sometimes irony fails, of course. "Kidding, kidding!" we may have to cry after saying something we wanted another person to turn around, but either the person failed to see that your expression needed turning, or you failed to give the person enough hints. When irony works, it helps to cement social bonds and mutual understanding because the speaker and hearer of irony both know to turn the utterance, and they know that the other one knows they will turn the utterance. When irony fails, it can be disastrous.

I am in the Big Brothers program, and I am White. Both my Little Brothers are African American. We are extremely close and have been for years. One day the younger of my brothers, while we were on an outing, asked if he could come back to my house afterward to hang out and download some tunes on my computer, to which I agreed. But half an hour later, he realized he had made another commitment that afternoon and told me he could not come to my house after all. "It's because I'm White, isn't it?" I said. He paused half a beat, then broke into a huge smile and said, "Yeah, that's it." Little exchanges like that are an ongoing part of our friendship. We both knew to turn the other's statement around. Now, had either one of us taken the other's expression literally, it would have been devastating to us. But because we know each other so well and have such a long history of kidding around, we knew instantly to turn the other's literal meaning. Irony worked in this case.

Notice that irony is heavily dependent on context. The social, physical, or historical context within which texts are placed can help readers know when to read something ironically. In the example above, my brother knows I am an ironic kind of guy who likes to joke around. Thus, he knew that a statement that would otherwise be outrageous ("It's because I'm White, isn't it?") was likely to be ironic coming from me—but perhaps not from some other people he might know. The context of our history together tells him that. When you make the crack about the length of the political speech in the example earlier in this section, you might help your friend to read your text as ironic by rolling your eyes, looking ostentatiously at your watch, sighing, and so forth. You are providing an immediate physical context to help your friend see your statement as ironic.

Texts themselves can create a context that signals the reader that irony is coming. You won't last long watching *The Daily Show* if you don't figure out from the text early on that pretty much everything is to be taken ironically. This helps you to read what comes next in the text. Readers look for cues that say, "Turn me! Don't take this literally!"

For instance, this book can be of great help to you in detecting irony. You must use it in a special way, though. First, it is important to stand only on your left foot. Go ahead, I'll wait while you stand like that. Now, you must balance this book, open to this page, on your head and repeat, "Neener, neener, neener" over and over until—okay, perhaps you get the picture. The first sentence of this paragraph was pretty straightforward. But as the paragraph progressed, the textual cues began piling up that you were to take everything following in the text as ironic. My intention was to construct this ironic context within the text fairly quickly. I hope the creation of this textual context for irony worked. If not, you can sit back down now.

There is a second sense of irony implied by Burke's statement, in overviewing the four master tropes, that for irony we may say *dialectic*.

What does he mean by *dialectic*? The term is ancient and has had several meanings throughout history, many of which overlap in Burke's usage. In the dialogues of the Greek philosopher Plato, dialectic was a discourse based on question and answer, the mutual interchange of views, with the goal of arriving at a shared understanding of the issue under discussion. In a later philosophical tradition, as in the work of the German philosopher Georg Wilhelm Friedrich Hegel, dialectic involved the idea of a thesis (some statement or stance), an antithesis (the opposite or denial of the thesis), and a synthesis (a way of thinking that merged thesis and antithesis in a transcendent understanding).

The common theme in both the Platonic and Hegelian sense of dialectic, and I believe it is also what Burke was emphasizing in saying that irony is dialectic, is the back-and-forth of two voices, stances, or perspectives that achieve an understanding. Many of the examples of irony we examined earlier are funny in a sarcastic way. *Merriam-Webster's Collegiate Dictionary* defines *sarcasm* as "a mode of satirical wit depending for its effect on bitter, caustic, and often ironic language that is usually directed against an individual." To see irony as dialectic is to see irony's core not as sarcasm or humor but as the back-and-forth of understanding that has to go on between people for irony to work. If you come in my door and stumble, and I smile and say, "That was graceful!" what makes that utterance ironic is not so much the sarcasm or humor as the fact that I know that you will know to turn my phrase away from the literal meaning—and you will know that I will know you should turn it—and so forth. You might go back through all the examples of irony we have discussed so far to consider how they all depend on that back-and-forth of understanding as much as they depend on humor, comedy, or sarcasm.

The rhetorical work of irony is to cement social bonds, and this happens precisely because of that back-and-forth understanding. Irony is a kind of winking at each other, as we all understand the game of meaning reversal that is being played. It is remarkable that this understanding can even occur with ancient or deceased authors, as when we read an ironic author who is long dead. For instance: "When I reflect upon the number of disagreeable people who I know who have gone to a better world, I am moved to lead a different life." Mark Twain wrote that long before you and I were born, in *Pudd'nhead Wilson's Calendar,* and it is clearly an ironic statement in which you can almost see him wink at us. If you think about it, it is amazing and intriguing that we can read a highly ironic author such as Twain, dead for a century, and know that he intends us to turn many of his statements and that he "knows" we will know, and so back and forth.

Figure 4.5

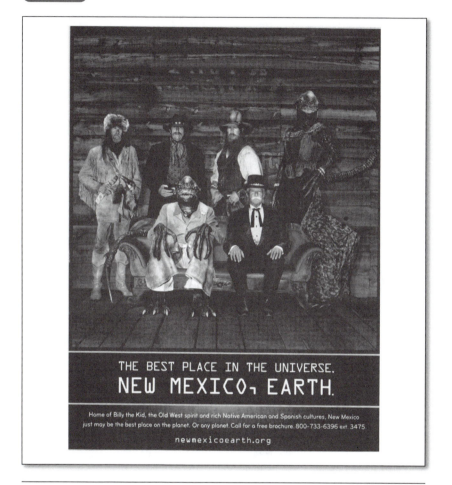

To view this image in full resolution, please visit www.sagepub.com/brummettstudy.

The close reader should therefore also be on the lookout for irony based on an understanding created dialectically with an audience, in addition to an irony that is sarcastic or humorous. Figure 4.5 illustrates this kind of irony. To make this advertisement for New Mexico "work," the reader must understand what the otherwise odd and unexplained references to other planets mean. The reader will think about Roswell, New Mexico, and Area 51, famed for alleged UFO visits. New Mexico is therefore alleged by some to be a place often visited by extraterrestrials! The reader will know that is what the creator of the text had in mind and that the creator intends the reader to draw that conclusion—and there you have a dialectic.

The classic Dire Straits rock-and-roll tune "Money for Nothing" is not especially humorous, but it is definitely ironic in a dialectical sense, as the audience is clearly meant to turn the group's song claiming that musicians get their money for nothing (and their chicks for free). We also know that Dire Straits will know that we know that we should turn the meanings of such an offensive claim—and so a dialectic is created. A similar dialectic may be found in Kanye West's song "Gold Digger," in which the audience is invited to share the singer's observations on relationships and exploitation through turning the meaning of the song's lyrics. A multipart exercise will help us to notice irony that depends on dialectic as much as it does humor or sarcasm.

EXERCISE 4.5

❖   Find some texts of a writer or speaker who is "preaching to the choir"—that is, addressing a group of highly like-minded people. Identify the extent to which the speaker or writer says something that the audience will understand in a very particular way because of their shared beliefs—and it is clear that the speaker knows the audience will have such an understanding, the speaker knows the audience will know the speaker expects such an understanding, and so forth. Political and religious speakers are good sources for such texts and may be found in many sources online or on television.

❖   Identify the extent to which this understanding between the speaker or writer and audience depends on some amount of turning of literal meaning—maybe not a total about-face, but some kind of bending of the meaning. If a religious speaker refers to "sinners" in a particular context, whom does the speaker expect the audience will take him to mean? Even a slight turning of an expression, from vagueness to specificity, can be ironic if a dialectic is created between author and audience.

❖   Consider the phenomenon of speaking "in code." Many people feel that if a speaker uses certain kinds of language, he or she is actually referring to some social group, political opinion, or public figure and that this will be very well understood by the audience. Thus, there are accusations that some politicians use "code" for race when they talk about the "problem of crime in our streets." In your class or among your friends are likely to be quite a few people who feel that such speaking or writing in code occurs frequently. Collect examples of these allegations, and notice the extent to which the texts require not only that the audience turn literal meanings somewhat but also that speaker and audience know that each intends the other to know that turning must occur—to know that a dialectic must be entered into. Think about how such a dialectic increases social bonds between authors and audiences.

❖ Some songwriters are more ironic than others, especially in the dialectic sense. Leonard Cohen is such an artist. Use an online search engine to find lyrics to his songs, which he has written over the span of several decades. Many musicians have recorded versions of his work. His song "Everybody Knows" has been recorded by him and by several other artists and is dialectical irony at its best. Study the song for ways in which a mutual understanding is created between the songwriter and the audience as his lyrics are turned.

❖ SUMMARY AND LOOKING AHEAD

In this chapter I have discussed *transformations:* ways in which the ordinary, literal meanings of signs and images are *turned*—reversed, changed, altered—by readers of texts. A close reader can learn much about how texts create meanings by looking at these ways in which ordinary meanings are turned.

A word for the kind of turning that occurs in transformations is *trope.* You learned that *a trope is a category of textual devices in which the literal, ordinary meaning of a sign or image must be turned or altered to arrive at what the sign or image means in a text.* The chapter is organized around the rhetorical theorist Kenneth Burke's scheme of *four master tropes,* which are *metaphor, metonymy, synecdoche,* and *irony.*

Metaphor speaks as if one thing were another thing when literally it is not. Burke tells us that the trope of metaphor creates a *perspective.* It uses a *tenor* and *vehicle* so that the vehicle helps us to see something about the tenor. We learned that a slightly weaker form of metaphor is *simile.* Simile says that the tenor is *like* or *as* the vehicle rather than equating the two. I stressed the importance of considering the *implications,* both intended and unintended, of a metaphor. I also noted that when implications are systematically developed, one has an *extended* metaphor.

Metonymy reduces an abstract idea to a concrete action, object, or event. Burke says that it is the trope of *reduction. Metonymy expresses an abstract idea in terms of something physical or material.* In searching for metonymies in texts, the close reader can ask whether signs of concrete actions, objects, and events may be reductions of broad, abstract ideas.

The close reader can also move in the other direction and begin with what he or she thinks are some abstract ideas expressed by a text and then look for signs of the concrete to which those ideas are reduced.

Synecdoche is the trope of *representation*. In synecdoche we refer to part of something when we mean the whole, because the part represents the whole. Or we can refer to whole for part, container for the thing contained, sign for the thing signified—we noted a range of synecdochic relationships named by Burke. In each case the close reader asks how the sign or image represents the action, object, or event to which it is connected.

Finally, we studied the trope of *irony*. Irony is sometimes taken to be the same thing as sarcasm and is often thought of as a humorous trope. You learned that irony often involves a complete *reversal* of the literal, ordinary meaning of an utterance, and when this happens, as on *The Daily Show*, the result is often comical. But we also noted Burke's equation of irony with *dialectic.* We noted that dialectic is key to a wider meaning of irony: the creation of an *exchange* between the speaker or writer and the reader of the text, in which each knows to turn the literal meaning of an utterance and in which each knows that the other will turn the utterance and that they are meant to do so. This kind of textual winking or creation of an interplay between parties to irony helps to cement social bonds, as people exercise their shared knowledge to arrive at an understanding.

I now turn to the fifth chapter in this survey of techniques of close reading. What we find in texts often has social and political importance. This works through the exercise of *argument* and *ideology*. In the next chapter, I explain techniques for identifying these concepts in texts.

5

Ideology and Argument

❖   ❖   ❖

Perhaps you have had a conversation with someone about another person, and your friend says to you, "Oh, she is very conservative." "How do you know?" you reply. At that point your friend may be at a loss for words but is still sure that the person you are discussing is conservative. Or liberal. Or feminist. Or fundamentalist. And so on and so forth. We often read whole ways of thinking and entire philosophies from what others say, do, and show us. Yet, we are often unclear about how we draw these conclusions or whether they are justified.

An interesting aspect of this kind of "mind reading" is that we seem to draw conclusions about what people think that go beyond the bare evidence presented to us. We could likely make a guess about a person's politics, religious leanings, and views on such issues as the environment, women's rights, military intervention, and so forth based on hearing their views on just a couple of items from this list. We might guess wrong, but many of us would venture a guess anyway. For instance, if you know that someone is in favor of banning offshore oil drilling, tighter controls over firearms, and reducing our military involvement overseas, you can probably make a good guess what they think about capital punishment and for whom they voted in the last election.

We take a chance on this "mind reading" because ways of thinking tend to be *systematic*—that is, certain kinds of values and convictions tend to be connected to others. People generally want their thinking to

.: consistent, and so what we think about the environment may well share some fundamental assumptions and values with what we think about government programs for the poor. Of course, we must remember that many people also harbor some attitudes at variance with their dominant ways of thinking.

When we conclude that someone is liberal, conservative, and so on, it seems clear that we have "read" something in what the person has done or said that leads us to conclude where he or she stands socially and politically. We know that such readings are not foolproof; sometimes we are surprised by a person's words or behaviors after we have made such a reading. I believe, though, that we can learn how to read more effectively the ways of thinking that people share. We can do this through the close reading of what I will shortly describe as *ideology*, and we read ideology through looking at *argument*.

For instance, consider this section of the main Web site for PETA, People for the Ethical Treatment of Animals:

WHY ANIMAL RIGHTS?

Almost all of us grew up eating meat, wearing leather, and going to circuses and zoos. We never considered the impact of these actions on the animals involved. For whatever reason, you are now asking the question: Why should animals have rights? LEARN MORE.

Animals Are Not Ours to Eat

Animals Are Not Ours to Wear

Animals Are Not Ours to Experiment On

Animals Are Not Ours to Use for Entertainment

Animals Are Not Ours to Abuse in Any Way

We see here a list of convictions and principles for this group. If we heard a speaker lay out these principles in a speech, I think most of us would guess that the speaker was also politically to the left, against capital punishment, in favor of simple living and respect for the environment—the list would go on. We might be wrong in such guesses, but I think more PETA proponents than not would share such stances. They just seem to "go with" a concern for animals' rights. How can we intentionally understand these networks of connected ideas? How can we read more carefully and intentionally—how can we do a close reading of—texts that seem to indicate wider systems of thought?

Let me call your attention to several important aspects of our readings of other people's thought.

- First, the webs of convictions and commitments that we identify can be called *ideology*. *Ideology* is one of those terms that varies considerably according to different theories. It is a term central to most variations on Marxist theory and method, for instance. Since we are focusing on techniques of close reading and not the theories that might guide those techniques, let me offer a generic definition of ideology that will serve our purposes and yet fit with most theories: *Ideology is a systematic network of beliefs, commitments, values, and assumptions that influence how power is maintained, struggled over, and resisted.* Other scholars offer similar generic understandings of the term. Suzanne Stewart-Steinberg tells us that "ideology is the mechanism by and through which individuals live their roles as subjects in a social formation" (185). Mark Lawrence McPhail sees the ideological as having to do with "how conflict, power, and material interests shape and influence social and symbolic interaction" (340). So our example of people from PETA would tell us that a belief in animal rights likely fits into a systematic network of beliefs and that these beliefs and commitments have something to do with how power in our society is created, struggled over, and resisted.

- A second aspect of drawing conclusions about people's social and political alignments is that in order to do so, we attend to the everyday *arguments* or *argumentation* (both terms are commonly used) that people employ in everyday speech, writing, and action. An argument faces in two directions: it tells us a speaker's ideology, but it also urges that ideology upon an audience. It is both a symptom and a creator of ideology. *Argument is a process by which speakers and writers, together with audiences, make claims about what people should do and assemble reasons and evidence why people should do those things.* Many scholars have studied argument and have arrived at similar definitions. Chaim Perelman and Lucie Olbrechts-Tyteca refer to argument in several ways: as "the domain of action of our faculty of reasoning and proving" (3) and as "techniques allowing us to induce or to increase the mind's adherence to the theses presented for its assent" (4). They claim that "all argumentation aims at gaining the adherence of minds" (14). Gary C. Woodward and Robert E. Denton, Jr., define argument as "claims linked to evidence or good reasons" (87). Stephen Toulmin, Richard Rieke, and Allan Janik define the closely related process of reasoning as "a collective and continuing human transaction, in which we present ideas or claims to particular sets of people within particular situations or contexts and offer the appropriate kinds of 'reasons' in their support" (9). If you visit the PETA Web site, you will see a fair bit of concern for the everyday messages people get that encourage the exploitation of animals, for such messages create the mindset that PETA would like to work against. In sum, ideology is the web of ideas people have, but argument is the materially observable discourse that both reveals a writer's ideology and urges that ideology on others.

- A third aspect of how we guess other people's ways of thinking is that although we are aware of our attributions of politics, religion, and so forth to others, we are not often consciously aware of how we make these attributions. This particular aspect of reading, in other words, is often *out of awareness*. Learning techniques of close reading can help us to see more clearly how people go about making assumptions about other people's ways of thinking based on their arguments. I believe that most of us, after spending a few minutes on the PETA Web site, would draw a number of conclusions about the further politics and lifestyle of members of that organization, even if we are not aware of the assumptions we are making.

Let me pull these considerations together at this point to talk about what I do in Chapter 5. This chapter will teach you some *techniques for closely reading* the everyday *arguments* in people's texts that reflect those people's ideologies. I proceed on the assumption that ideology is largely created, maintained, and resisted in *everyday* argument, more so than in grand, single moments of indoctrination and persuasion. If you think about your own ideologies, I believe you will realize that they sort of seeped into your head over a lifetime of hearing the everyday arguments of others. Or if, as is sometimes the case, you have recently resisted or rejected some ideology, that decision is usually the result of a long process of weighing everyday arguments, rather than the result of any single dramatic experience.

❖ FOUR QUESTIONS TO ASK ABOUT A TEXT

When we learn how to read other people's ideologies, then, we are learning about the rhetorical environment that is created around us. We therefore learn something about how we might create, sustain, or resist ideologies ourselves. This is because the arguments that call others to think, feel, and act in some ways are likely also calling to us. In an important sense, to learn to understand the role of everyday arguments in creating ideologies is to learn how social and individual consciousness is shaped. The chapter is organized around these four questions, which the close reader should ask about the arguments in a text under examination:

- What should the audience think or do?
- What does the text ask the audience to assume?
- How does the audience know what the text claims?
- Who is empowered or disempowered?

From asking these questions about argument, we may draw some conclusions about ideology. Let's consider these four questions one by one.

What Should the Audience Think or Do?

When we ask what the reader should think or do, we are asking what claims or conclusions the text would lead to. Sometimes these are not spelled out, and a value of close reading is to make the implied claims of the text clear so that audiences may know what they are buying into with that text. What the audience should think or do may sometimes end up going well beyond the particular subject of the argument—the claim may affect wide ranges of thought and action. The interconnectedness of ideology, the fact that it is a network of ideas, means that placing one idea in an audience's head often makes it easier for the audience to go on to another idea.

To ask someone to think or do a thing implies a wider moral or ethical standard that the thought or action supports. If I ask you to contribute to wildlife preservation, that implies acceptance of a wider standard, one of caring for animals and for the natural world. Our first question should encourage readers to think about the wider networks of thought implied by the specific call to thought or action in a text. Such a wider network is, as we saw earlier, an ideology. Even an advertisement urging the reader to buy mouthwash implies, by calling for that action, a wider network of thought. To buy mouthwash leads us to think that good health and hygiene involve smelling good, smelling a particular way. Of course, the ideology also implies that we achieve these standards through spending money and buying a product; this wider network of ideas is ideological.

What Does the Text Ask the Audience to Assume?

Every argument must begin with some assumptions. Even the call "Run! The house is on fire!" must be based on such assumptions as the danger of fire, the need to flee to avoid fire, the idea that human bodies cannot withstand fire, and so forth. When we ask about assumptions, we are asking what both the writer or speaker and the audience for the text bring to an argument to make it "work." These assumptions tend to be connected in a network, and that network is ideological. If our first question leads us to think about the ideology that comes from an argument, this second question leads us to think about the ideology, the network of ideas, that an audience must already have so as to make sense of an argument.

Most news reports on the state of the economy assume that growth is good, and that is connected to other assumptions, such as the idea that people are supposed to use and exploit the earth's resources, that more and bigger are always better, that poverty is a source of shame, and so forth. You need to share that assumption, or the argument won't "work" for you. An idea widely held among professors is the belief that plagiarism, or use of another's words as if they were one's own, is a serious academic offense. But many students do not come to school sharing that assumption in the first place, and so warnings against plagiarism by professors often make no sense or fall on deaf ears. Professors often work to instill this assumption in students so that future appeals to avoid plagiarism will work.

Another way to think about this second question is to ask what the text takes for granted. What does the text seem to assume that the audience already agrees with? The close reader might think about how the substance of the text would be different were it addressed to a different audience. Study a president's recent State of the Union message, for instance. What does the speech assume that it could likely not assume if addressed to the Mexican people or to the Canadian parliament? Your answer to that question will help to reveal the ideology the text already takes for granted as it approaches an audience, as it calls to an audience, assumed to share that ideology.

Often a text's assumptions make it appear as if everybody in the world shared them. The assumptions of an ideology often seem universal in that way to those who share the ideology. It can be instructive to study a text from a quite different time or place, to identify assumptions taken to be universal in that text but which you, the reader, do not share. Some texts in defense of slavery written by early-nineteenth-century American slaveholders might be a good place to detect assumptions precisely because those assumptions are not shared today. Today, texts having to do with the rights of gay, lesbian, bisexual, and transgendered people may be fruitfully studied for their assumptions precisely because different audiences in the United States do not share assumptions and ideologies concerning those issues.

Another way to get at the question of assumptions is to think about what the text takes to be "natural" or "common sense." These are terms for assumptions. Most text, to pursue our example of the last paragraph, assume that if one is speaking of a "family," one is speaking of a mother, a father, and their biological offspring. There is thus a widespread ideology in American society, although surely not one universally shared, that families are naturally and commonsensically based on heterosexual couples.

How Does the Audience Know What the Text Claims?

The assumptions of ideology made by a text are different from the evidence the text offers for its claims. In probing this question, we want to know how the reader knows what the text claims. What does a text do to lead the reader to that knowledge?

Our earlier question about assumptions may point us toward this question of evidence because assumptions form the *standards of proof* that evidence must meet. A speaker and an audience may share the assumption that whatever is found in a particular religious text must be true. The speaker and audience thus share a religious ideology. If that is the standard of proof for that ideology, that points toward the kind of evidence the text will present to lead the audience to knowledge of the text's claims. If being found in the Koran is the standard of proof for one ideology, then actual quotations from the Koran can function as evidence, leading the audience to knowledge.

In addition to using the assumptions of an audience, a text usually offers evidence, or "proof," for what it asks the audience to do or think. What counts as evidence varies widely and can be quite revealing the ideological implications of a text. Think of the ideological di ences between a text that offers Biblical passages as evidence an that quotes recent scientific studies as evidence—this is not only a matter of proof but a matter of urging one ideology or another upon an audience. The mere citing of either Biblical or scientific evidence invokes the whole network of beliefs that is an ideology.

As a close reader you might look at "true crime" shows on television, especially those that send a camera to follow actual police around for a night. Ask yourself what assumptions are made by the texts of these shows, what ideology and standards of proof they assume are shared by the producers of the show and the audience. And then ask yourself what kind of evidence the shows produce to suggest certain ideas to the audience. For instance, is the audience generally urged to think that those detained or arrested are guilty of crimes? Does the text assume a shared ideology in which the police are generally correct and justified in their actions? Think about the evidence given in the shows that lead the audience to mutter, "Guilty, guilty, guilty!" Why does that evidence "work" in the shows? How does it meet certain standards of evidence? My point here is not to criticize the shows or the police but rather to ask you to examine the ideology implied and perpetuated by these shows.

Who Is Empowered or Disempowered?

Finally, we should ask who is empowered or disempowered by a text. An ideological close reading assumes that power is always at work to some extent in a text, and understanding how the text connects to structures and struggles over power helps to reveal its ideological import. Even an advertisement for soup empowers the people selling soup; depending on the text, it may empower homemakers by promising more free time, or it may disempower homemakers by constraining their thoughts about how to live life alone within the home. The network of ideas that is an ideology usually creates the same empowerments and disempowerments across the web of connected ideas.

Some kinds of empowerment relate to presence or absence: what ideas, what sorts of people, what ways of life or habits of thought, are shown and are not shown. Only in the last few decades have gay, les-
᠎ ansgendered people begin to appear on television
᠎s. Only in the last few decades have interracial cou-
᠎xts of popular culture. In an even more recent time
᠎ become more widely visible. Visibility is empower-
᠎s disempowerment, and readers should ask of texts
᠎d who is "absent." The same question may be asked
ystems of thought, of course.

Another way to get at empowerment is to ask what sort of hierarchies are implied by the text: who it says ought to "be in charge" and who not. Over the last several decades, children and young people appear to be more empowered in texts of popular culture. In the 1950s, children on television or in film would ask their parents for permission to do any little thing. Nowadays, you don't need to look for long at shows on children's cable television channels to find almost an absence of parents and parental authority. This certainly bespeaks a shift in empowerment and disempowerment.

❖ PUTTING OUR QUESTIONS TOGETHER:
   A BRIEF EXAMPLE

Let us look at a brief example of an ordinary text found in everyday experience and how the ideology and arguments in the text might be opened up through a close reading based on those questions. I was watching a television show the other day on hauntings—cable television seems to be full of such programs—and someone whose home was allegedly haunted offered an argument for the reality of ghosts. It went something like this:

> Everybody is made of energy, and you can't destroy energy. So when someone dies, their energy continues on, and that's what a ghost is. We are seeing, hearing, and feeling someone's energy after their death.

Our four questions need not be applied to this sort of close reading in the order listed. Often, one question will lead us into the text more fruitfully than others, and sometimes several questions pop up at once. Let's begin with the "evidence" question: How does the audience know what the text claims? The speaker offered no more information than what you see above. Energy is a concept in physics, for which there have been centuries of scientific study, yet none of that evidence is given in the statement. The speaker seems to assume that the audience—to bring in another of our questions—believes that the human being or essence is fundamentally energy. How is that assumption bolstered? How do we know what the speaker says? For one thing, it sounds "sort of" true that energy cannot be destroyed. Didn't we all hear someplace that if you shine a flashlight into the sky, the light keeps going forever (although it dissipates more with every mile it travels)? The speaker has, in other words, alluded to what the audience may vaguely recall as a possibly correct statement about physics, so as to encourage the reader to *assume* that the statement "we are all energy" is *factually* correct. It is close enough to what we may have read in a physics textbook to make the uncritical listener accept it as fact. Later, I refer to this kind of "knowledge" as "folk science."

Clearly, what the audience is to think or do (another of our questions) is to believe in the reality of ghostly hauntings, in the existence of human life and consciousness after death, and in the claim that it is just such a ghost that is creating the disturbances in the speaker's home. Note that even if it were true that energy continues, the speaker must ask the audience to assume that the energy that was part of one human being continues in some organized form after death such that one could see a figure floating through a room and exclaim, "Oh my! It's Larry!" People in her house thought they were seeing recognizable human forms, after all, not mere blobs or light. Not only are we asked to think that "energy" that is recognizable as Larry or any other deceased person continues to be organized (rather than, like our flashlight beam, dispersing into entropic chaos), we are also asked to assume that this sort of ghost would retain some level of intentionality: in other words, that the energy retains the intention to float through the room, appearing to the room's occupants.

The argument is therefore asking readers to think that we, after death, may likewise continue in an organized and intentional form. This is not surprising, nor is it different from claims made by many religions. What is interesting ideologically about this claim is that it is *not* made on the basis of spiritual or religious evidence. What for centuries and in many contexts would be a religious argument (e.g., "the soul continues after death") is made here as a scientific argument. This leads us to the question we have not yet considered, that of empowerment. It's clear that statements like this would contribute to empowering institutions of science more than institutions of religion. It does not depend on the priests, rabbis, or enlightened ones for validation. But does it shift validation to scientists? No; because the speaker did not reference specific scientific studies, which might be sponsored by institutions of science, what is really referenced is ordinary people's "everyday" sense of science. We all have what we might call a "folk science" in our heads: no two snowflakes are alike, hot water freezes into ice cubes faster than cold water does, and so forth. The empowerment in the speaker's statement then has nothing to do directly with ghosts but instead has to do with our settled ideas of *folk* scientific "truth" (which may be true but may also be crackpot).

That empowerment of ordinary people's ideas of everyday science may give us pause in the end. People may have all sorts of ideas they think are scientifically grounded because they read them in tabloid newspapers or heard them in comedy-show jokes or got them from family lore. These ideas can feed into ideologies, some of which may be questionable or downright harmful. All sorts of racist or sexist ideologies are based on pseudoscientific notions of mental ability and character flaws grounded in exactly that sort of folk science. Your cranky uncle may solemnly repeat that the brain sizes of certain races are smaller or that the physical capabilities of women are inferior, based on that kind of folk science.

The speaker's statement seems harmless enough. Let her believe in ghosts if she likes, and let her urge that belief on others. But to couch her belief in the terms that she does furthers an ideology that can have unpleasant consequences in other matters beyond the supernatural. It can coach an attitude toward what counts as scientific data that ends up supporting such unsavory ideologies as racism, sexism, and the like. We need to be careful when such ideologies are supported.

❖ THREE EXAMPLES FOR CLOSE READING

Now we turn to "thicker" texts that offer meatier chances to analyze arguments and the ideologies they support. As our chief objects of study in this chapter, I offer three examples for the close reading of argument and ideology, Figures 5.1, 5.2, and 5.3. They make an interesting range of texts. The first may seem like an unusual choice for a reader in the twenty-first century: the British poet Rudyard Kipling's poem "Tommy" from 1892. The Tommy in the poem is a British soldier, and in the poem Kipling, speaking through the accent and vernacular language of the soldier, makes an argument about how a society treats its ordinary soldiers. When you read it, you may be surprised by some parallels with our situation today, in which many have complained that the ordinary man or woman in uniform is called upon to make great sacrifice without sufficient support or respect from his or her country. Figure 5.2 is an article, "Only Connect," from the *New York Times Magazine*. It argues that wealthy tourists are seeking out opportunities to "connect" with ordinary people around the globe during vacation trips. These tourists sign up for "reality tours," and the author seems to be saying that such adventures allow the tourist to make an "authentic" connection. Finally, Figure 5.3 is an article from a Web site

opposed to same-sex marriages: http://www.nogaymarriage.com/
tenarguments.asp. The article is a summary of a book by noted evangelist Dr. James Dobson. It gives ten reasons to oppose same-sex marriage and is an excellent extended example of a complex argument
with great ideological impact. Let us now turn to our first in-depth
example, the poem "Tommy."

"Tommy"

Figure 5.1

Tommy

Rudyard Kipling

I went into a public-'ouse to get a pint o' beer,
The publican 'e up an' sez, "We serve no red-coats here."
The girls be'ind the bar they laughed an' giggled fit to die,
I outs into the street again an' to myself sez I:
    O it's Tommy this, an' Tommy that, an' "Tommy, go away";
    But it's "Thank you, Mister Atkins", when the band begins to play,
    The band begins to play, my boys, the band begins to play,
    O it's "Thank you, Mister Atkins", when the band begins to play.

I went into a theatre as sober as could be,
They gave a drunk civilian room, but 'adn't none for me;
They sent me to the gallery or round the music-'alls,
But when it comes to fightin', Lord! they'll shove me in the stalls!
    For it's Tommy this, an' Tommy that, an' "Tommy, wait outside";
    But it's "Special train for Atkins" when the trooper's on the tide,
    The troopship's on the tide, my boys, the troopship's on the tide,
    O it's "Special train for Atkins" when the trooper's on the tide.

Yes, makin' mock o' uniforms that guard you while you sleep
Is cheaper than them uniforms, an' they're starvation cheap;
An' hustlin' drunken soldiers when they're goin' large a bit
Is five times better business than paradin' in full kit.
    Then it's Tommy this, an' Tommy that, an' "Tommy, 'ow's yer soul?"
    But it's "Thin red line of 'eroes" when the drums begin to roll,
    The drums begin to roll, my boys, the drums begin to roll,
    O it's "Thin red line of 'eroes" when the drums begin to roll.

We aren't no thin red 'eroes, nor we aren't no blackguards too,
But single men in barricks, most remarkable like you;
An' if sometimes our conduck isn't all your fancy paints,
Why, single men in barricks don't grow into plaster saints;

While it's Tommy this, an' Tommy that, an' "Tommy, fall be'ind",
But it's "Please to walk in front, sir", when there's trouble in the wind,
There's trouble in the wind, my boys, there's trouble in the wind,
O it's "Please to walk in front, sir", when there's trouble in the wind.

You talk o' better food for us, an' schools, an' fires, an' all:
We'll wait for extry rations if you treat us rational.
Don't mess about the cook-room slops, but prove it to our face
The Widow's Uniform is not the soldier-man's disgrace.
    For it's Tommy this, an' Tommy that, an' "Chuck him out, the brute!"
    But it's "Saviour of 'is country" when the guns begin to shoot;
    An' it's Tommy this, an' Tommy that, an' anything you please;
    An' Tommy ain't a bloomin' fool — you bet that Tommy sees!

In terms of argument, the poem "Tommy" is what is sometimes called an enthymeme. The enthymeme was first theorized in ancient Greece. It is the sort of everyday argument we use to help us make decisions in matters where we cannot be certain. It is sometimes thought of as an "incomplete" argument because the audience is expected to supply key parts of the argument. If I tell you, "Buy tomatoes at the next store; they are cheaper there," that is an enthymeme because, although I offer a claim (buy tomatoes at the next store) and a reason (they are cheaper there), I count on you, my audience, to fill in the parts of the argument that would say that cheaper is better, that the next store is near enough to make it easy to go there, and so forth. Because the audience must fill in parts of the argument, enthymemes rely on widely held social knowledge.

"Tommy" is an enthymeme because it depends on social knowledge. As a poem we would not expect it to quote the latest statistics or a recent newspaper story to make a case that those in uniform are unfairly treated. "Tommy" does not cite this morning's CNN lead story. Instead, it makes use of what "everybody knows." The episodes of humiliation for soldiers and sailors that it reports will make sense to the audience precisely because it has witnessed those episodes— perhaps, to its shame, the audience has engaged in such behavior. The question of how the audience knows the truth of the stories told in the poem is then answered with the audience's own experience.

The poem consists of little vignettes, moments of drama strung together, each one with a moral attached. The audience had likely seen or heard of episodes such as the one in the first stanza, in which soldiers are denied service and laughed at in uniform. Readers of the poem may have witnessed an event such as the one in the second stanza, where the soldier is turned away from a theater, but drunken civilians are welcomed in. There is special room for him on the troop train going to war but not in a theater. Note that every single stanza and each refrain contain phrases in quotation marks. This drives the point home to the reader by referencing something once actually said and said again now. So the audience is asked to attest to the truth of these "quotations" and stories, as having heard them or something like them in the audience's own experience.

One reason enthymemes work powerfully as argument is that they involve the audience, which brings to the argument what it needs for completion. The audience helps the arguer along just by filling in parts. *Assumptions* behind the argument are a major part of what the audience must bring to "Tommy." The assumptions most likely to be referenced by these arguments concern how class worked in the British social system of the nineteenth century. But the poem works for today's audiences to the extent that we share some of those assumptions of class.

The most important assumption based on class is that the soldiers in the poem are of lower socioeconomic class. England in the nineteenth century was highly stratified by class, and everybody was aware of how class was marked. To read the poem as Kipling intended in the nineteenth century required the audience to apply assumptions it held about markers of class. It is surprising how much today's reader of the poem will bring the same assumptions to the reading. And in fact, our military today recruits a disproportionately large percentage of its force from those with less money and fewer economic opportunities.

Beer is historically seen as a drink for the common person, and that was certainly the case when "Tommy" was written. Tommy goes into a bar for beer. He is turned away from the main part of the theater but is sent to the balcony (or gallery) or to music halls, which would have been recognized as sites of entertainment for the lower classes. Tommy's banishment to the gallery, or balcony, brings to mind the scandalous banishment of African Americans to the balconies of movie theaters during decades of Jim Crow laws and segregation. Thus the poem may have ideological impact beyond military examples.

Tommy's language will have been widely read as lower class. Kipling ensures this assumption by introducing errors in spelling that are also meant to signal lower-class or cockney pronunciation. The *h* is dropped in "public-'ouse" as well as in "'e" in the next line and "be'ind" two lines after that, and beyond. It's "sez" and not *says*. In the third stanza and elsewhere, *g* is dropped in "makin,'" "hustlin,'" and "goin.'"

Other markers of class are the cheapness of the uniforms, the poor quality of food ("cook-room slops"), and the nearly unlivable conditions of the "barricks," which evidently were in want of heat or "fire." Tommy and his fellow soldiers are more likely to be from the lower classes if adults like them are in want of "schools," which the poem says are promised but not delivered. These examples are offered as evidence in support of the argument, but they also invoke the assumptions the reader would need to make to recognize that Tommy is of a lower economic class. This poem still resonates with many today who may complain that wars take advantage of men and women from lower economic classes, some of whom may enlist because of poor job prospects elsewhere. Even for those who enlist out of patriotism and pride of country today, complaints of poor supplies, equipment, and housing sound like many headlines today from our country's military conflicts around the world. Soldiers are of a lower economic class once they enlist, even if they were not before, and audiences know how to read the class status from the examples given.

An interesting assumption concerning morality and class is invoked. A common assumption in nineteenth-century England was that the lower classes were less moral and less ethical. Note the couplet,

> An' if sometimes our conduck isn't all your fancy paints,
> Why, single men in barricks don't grow into plaster saints;

This argument invokes the reader's assumption that the lower classes are not "saints" yet gives a reason for it: the living conditions ("Single men in barricks") of the lower classes. The assumption is invoked to give a reason why it may be true but is not a failing of the lower classes.

"Tommy" seems to be an attempt to empower the common soldier, then, at least through calling his or her plight to public attention. The poem is in a position to urge a change in public attitudes about men and women in uniform and to encourage soldiers by giving voice to some of their grievances. It is a cry of shame upon those who would have soldiers "walk in front" in times of danger but step to the rear in times of peace. As a poem, it will be read across time and space. What it asks the reader to think or do is therefore something that the reader must bring to the poem in addition to evidence and assumptions. This is an enthymeme even in what it asks of the reader; the poem's point or bottom line must be filled in by the audience.

A reading of action, attitude, and empowerment would not be complete without considering this reservation, however: in empowering the lower socioeconomic classes, the poem also replicates and reinscribes conditions used by the powerful to keep the lower classes in check. The poem does *not* show us that Tommy violates assumptions about the lower classes as less educated and articulate, as sometimes immoral or unruly, as sometimes materially wretched. It lays the blame for these conditions at the door of the powerful, and it is a powerful argument for humanity and acceptance of the lower classes, but it reinforces rather than breaks any stereotypes. It may have to do so if it works by invoking some stereotypes that are in the audience's minds as assumptions and evidence. This difficult balance between marking any group that is disadvantaged—because of sex, sexuality, race, age, and so forth—and challenging the markers themselves is often found in arguments that attempt to change conditions of power.

"Only Connect"

Figure 5.2

The article "Only Connect," by Anna Louie Sussman, appeared in *The New York Times Magazine.* This magazine, like its host newspaper, is in business to make money. It makes money as the national "newspaper of record," as the most respected daily newspaper in the nation's largest city. New York is also one of the wealthiest cities in the country and thus very much into making money itself. The articles, the editorials, the advertisements all bespeak a certain level of moneyed sophistication. Of course, ordinary people read the *Times,* but stylistically it presents itself as very uptown. It speaks to people who have financial means, and much of its content, whether on style, sports, entertainment, or travel, advises these folks on how to spend their money.

"Only Connect," too, indirectly asks its audience to spend money, on the sort of tour described in the article. The subtitle describes those who take the tour as "people who need people." In fact, the tourists described are also people who need tax shelters and certified public accountants. In many ways, this article is the flip side of "Tommy." It addresses those who would be in a position to have "dinner with a maharajah" and titillates the rest of us by showing us how that richer group lives. In sum, "Only Connect" purveys an ideology of shopping, and the product in this case is the experience of different human beings.

One need not get far beyond the "people who need people" subtitle to see that those who are taking tours like this one "need people" in the sense that one might "need" a new BMW: one goes out and buys one. It is clear in the first place that the article assumes these tourists are well to do. How do we know this? What evidence is offered?

The article is clear: the first sentence references "affluent travelers," the sort who can afford "a private villa and an after-hours museum tour." These are people used to "a bubble of luxury." They are used to beluga caviar. A representative occupation mentioned for these tourists is that of doctor. Notice also the fascinating statement that "'[p]eople are looking to enrich themselves'" through these tours. Of course, one must be rich to begin with to afford such a thing, but the sort of experience with local people that is offered is described as a way to enrich oneself. Getting richer is the gold standard, so to speak, by which these tours are measured—they are a good investment, just like one's mutual funds.

A significant key to the ideology of the article is a major assumption that is never questioned here: that human connection can be bought. First, let us note the poignancy of the statement that "a cult of authenticity has taken hold among global nomads." I don't think they worry so about having authentic experiences on the South Side of Chicago, the South Bronx, or other economically disadvantaged districts. This "moneyed set" has, in the argument of the article, an unmet need for authentic human connection. We might pause and consider ways in which that "bubble of luxury" leads to a yearning for authenticity, or "culture unfiltered," as the article puts it—how wealth can isolate one and create a sense of artificiality in one's life. This yearning is such that "'[t]hey're willing to sacrifice, say, the plunge pool and go to a place like Swaziland.'" Swaziland is evidently authentic, one of several sites of these "reality tours."

But this authenticity can be purchased specifically through these tours—human connection is for sale. One would think the wealthy could simply go visit their gardeners or stroll down the streets of the rough parts of their own towns, but that kind of real experience would not be commodified. These tours specifically offer authenticity for sale. One purchases the human connection, and an important dimension of this authenticity is precisely this assumption that such connection *can* be bought and sold.

It is clear that it is human connection, or in some sense the humans themselves, that is for sale. Of the tour company president we learn,

> . . . Zack encourages local guides to take guests back to their villages. "We want them to say, 'Hey, meet my great-aunt, she's 92. Meet my 24 cousins . . .'"

This is explicitly described as "luxury travel" that gives one "the human touch." Among the real human experiences you might have are "trips through the Argentinean pampa with a band of guitar-strumming gauchos." That it is human connection for sale in hopes of authenticity is clear. This travel trend is called "the new humanism."

A language of commodification, of buying and selling, is very much apparent in the article. A standard sales pitch, for instance, is that the product on sale is rare or about to run out: "Three days only! Once they are sold, they are gone! Never again at this price!" And that is precisely what we find in this statement: "'People are sensing that stuff is going,' she says. 'Not just places but people.'" Note the merging of places and people alike into "stuff," or commodities: go to Swaziland now, you won't be able to buy the "stuff" of human connection like this much longer.

The purchase of authenticity and human contact goes only so far. One may go to Swaziland, one may meet a "local" grandmother, but to actually spend the night—to share food and drink, to share intimate space—the article promises the bubble of luxury again. Note that the examples of "home stays" are not in Swaziland but with "the heirs of the stately Clonalis House in Country Roscommon, Ireland, or the well-connected owners of Ballyvolane, a manor in County Cork." The tourist may meet the twenty-four cousins in Swaziland but then beat it back to the lodge before sunset.

What the article wants the reader to do is, of course, to take the tour. It's not explicitly an advertisement, but it works like one and was surely written with the support and encouragement of the tour companies. More significantly, the article perpetuates an ideology of privileged wealth that purchases anything it wants, including human connection. Luxury will not be denied and keeps sneaking through. You might make an "educational" connection with poor villagers, but when it comes time to "bunk down" for the night, it's not the straw in a hut but the five-hundred-thread-count sheets at the manor that are substituted at the last minute for authenticity.

How ironic the title, then: "Only Connect." That is what we do when we purchase a commodity: we are not looking for a lifelong personal connection with that new rug, we only want to connect with it, to buy it, to have it around. The local people, many of them likely poor, are not permanently befriended. No real commitment is asked of the wealthy tourist. The tourist tries to "only connect," and then it's jetting back off to the penthouse suite to tell friends about it over that beluga caviar. As it perpetuates an ideology of the good life through consumption, the tours lead the wealthy into the same trap of inauthenticity from which they were trying to escape. At some level even those living in a "bubble of luxury" must know that stroking human commodities in this way cannot lead to authentic connection. No commodification can, but if that is the basis for one's ideology, one's lifestyle, one will have a yearning that can never be filled. Solutions are never bought but really only rented temporarily—by taking the tours.

"Gay Marriage: Why Would It Affect Me? Ten Arguments Against Same Sex Marriage"

Figure 5.3

Gay Marriage: Why Would It Affect Me?

Ten Arguments Against Same Sex Marriage

(This is a synopsis of the new book by
Dr. James Dobson, *Marriage Under Fire*.)

Argument #1

The implications for children in a world of decaying families are profound.
A recent article in the Weekly Standard described how the advent of legally
sanctioned gay unions in Scandinavian countries has already destroyed the
institution of marriage, where half of today's children are born out of wedlock.

(Continued)

(Continued)

It is predicted now, based on demographic trends in this country, that more than half of the babies born in the 1990s will spend at least part of their childhood in single-parent homes.

Social scientists have been surprisingly consistent in warning against this fractured family. If it continues, almost every child will have several "moms" and "dads," perhaps six or eight "grandparents," and dozens of half-siblings. It will be a world where little boys and girls are shuffled from pillar to post in an ever-changing pattern of living arrangements-where huge numbers of them will be raised in foster-care homes or living on the street (as millions do in other countries all over the world today). Imagine an environment where nothing is stable and where people think primarily about themselves and their own self-preservation.

The apostle Paul described a similar society in Romans 1, which addressed the epidemic of homosexuality that was rampant in the ancient world and especially in Rome at that time. He wrote, "They have become filled with every kind of wickedness, evil, greed and depravity. They are full of envy, murder, strife, deceit and malice. They are gossips, slanderers, God-haters, insolent, arrogant and boastful; they invent ways of doing evil; they disobey their parents; they are senseless, faithless, heartless, ruthless" (v. 29-31, NIV).

It appears likely now that the demise of families will accelerate this type of decline dramatically, resulting in a chaotic culture that will be devastating to children.

Argument #2

The introduction of legalized gay marriages will lead inexorably to polygamy and other alternatives to one-man, one-woman unions.

In Utah, polygamist Tom Green, who claims five wives, is citing Lawrence v. Texas as the legal authority for his appeal. This past January, a Salt Lake City civil rights attorney filed a federal lawsuit on behalf of another couple wanting to engage in legal polygamy. Their justification? Lawrence v. Texas.

The ACLU of Utah has actually suggested that the state will "have to step up to prove that a polygamous relationship is detrimental to society"-as opposed to the polygamists having to prove that plural marriage is not harmful to the culture. Do you see how the game is played? Despite 5,000 years of history, the burden now rests on you and me to prove that polygamy is unhealthy. The ACLU went on to say that the nuclear family "may not be necessarily the best model." Indeed, Justice Antonin Scalia warned of this likelihood in his statement for the minority in the Lawrence case.10 It took less than six months for his prediction to become reality.

Why will gay marriage set the table for polygamy?   Because there is no place to stop once that Rubicon has been crossed. Historically, the definition of marriage has rested on a bedrock of tradition, legal precedent, theology and the overwhelming support of the people.

After the introduction of marriage between homosexuals, however, it will be supported by nothing more substantial than the opinion of a single judge or by a black-robed panel of justices. After they have done their wretched work, the family will consist of little more than someone's interpretation of "rights."

Given that unstable legal climate, it is certain that some self-possessed judge, somewhere, will soon rule that three men and one woman can marry. Or five and two, or four and four. Who will be able to deny them that right? The guarantee is implied, we will be told, by the Constitution. Those who disagree will continue to be seen as hate-mongers and bigots. (Indeed, those charges are already being leveled against those of us who espouse biblical values!) How about group marriage, or marriage between relatives, or marriage between adults and children? How about marriage between a man and his donkey? Anything allegedly linked to "civil rights" will be doable. The legal underpinnings for marriage will have been destroyed.

Argument #3

An even greater objective of the homosexual movement is to end the state's compelling interest in marital relationships altogether. After marriages have been redefined, divorces will be obtained instantly, will not involve a court, and will take on the status of a driver's license or a hunting permit. With the family out of the way, all rights and privileges of marriage will accrue to gay and lesbian partners without the legal entanglements and commitments heretofore associated with it.

Argument #4

With the legalization of homosexual marriage, every public school in the nation will be required to teach that this perversion is the moral equivalent of traditional marriage between a man and a woman. Textbooks, even in conservative states, will have to depict man/man and woman/woman relationships, and stories written for children as young as elementary school, or even kindergarten, will have to give equal space to homosexuals.

Argument #5

From that point forward, courts will not be able to favor a traditional family involving one man and one woman over a homosexual couple in matters of adoption. Children will be placed in homes with parents representing only one sex on an equal basis with those having a mom and a dad. The prospect of fatherless and motherless children will not be considered in the evaluation of eligibility. It will be the law.

Argument #6

Foster-care parents will be required to undergo "sensitivity training" to rid themselves of bias in favor of traditional marriage, and will have to affirm homosexuality in children and teens.

(Continued)

(Continued)

Argument #7

How about the impact on Social Security if there are millions of new dependents that will be entitled to survivor benefits? It will amount to billions of dollars on an already overburdened system. And how about the cost to American businesses? Unproductive costs mean fewer jobs for those who need them. Are state and municipal governments to be required to raise taxes substantially to provide health insurance and other benefits to millions of new "spouses and other dependents"?

Argument #8

Marriage among homosexuals will spread throughout the world, just as pornography did after the Nixon Commission declared obscene material "beneficial" to mankind.11 Almost instantly, the English-speaking countries liberalized their laws against smut. America continues to be the fountainhead of filth and immorality, and its influence is global.

The point is that numerous leaders in other nations are watching to see how we will handle the issue of homosexuality and marriage. Only two countries in the world have authorized gay marriage to date-the Netherlands and Belgium. Canada is leaning in that direction, as are numerous European countries. Dr. Darrell Reid, president of Focus on the Family Canada, told me two weeks ago that his country is carefully monitoring the United States to see where it is going. If we take this step off a cliff, the family on every continent will splinter at an accelerated rate. Conversely, our U.S. Supreme Court has made it clear that it looks to European and Canadian law in the interpretation of our Constitution.13 What an outrage! That should have been grounds for impeachment, but the Congress, as usual, remained passive and silent.

Argument #9

Perhaps most important, the spread of the Gospel of Jesus Christ will be severely curtailed. The family has been God's primary vehicle for evangelism since the beginning.

Its most important assignment has been the propagation of the human race and the handing down of the faith to our children. Malachi 2:15 reads, referring to husbands and wives, "Has not the Lord made them one? In flesh and spirit they are His. And why one? Because He was seeking godly offspring. So guard yourself in your spirit, and do not break faith with the wife of your youth" (NIV).

That responsibility to teach the next generation will never recover from the loss of committed, God-fearing families. The younger generation and those yet to come will be deprived of the Good News, as has already occurred in France, Germany and other European countries. Instead of providing for a father and mother, the advent of homosexual marriage will create millions of motherless children and fatherless kids. This is morally wrong, and is condemned in Scripture. Are we now going to join the Netherlands and Belgium to become the third country in the history of the world to "normalize" and legalize behavior that has been prohibited by God himself? Heaven help us if we do!

Argument #10

The culture war will be over, and I fear, the world may soon become "as it was in the days of Noah" (Matthew 24:37, NIV). This is the climactic moment in the battle to preserve the family, and future generations hang in the balance.

  This apocalyptic and pessimistic view of the institution of the family and its future will sound alarmist to many, but I think it will prove accurate unless-unless-God's people awaken and begin an even greater vigil of prayer for our nation. That's why Shirley and I are urgently seeking the Lord's favor and asking Him to hear the petitions of His people and heal our land.

  As of this time, however, large segments of the church appear to be unaware of the danger; its leaders are surprisingly silent about our peril (although we are tremendously thankful for the efforts of those who have spoken out on this issue). The lawless abandon occurring recently in California, New Mexico, New York, Oregon, Washington and elsewhere should have shocked us out of our lethargy. So far, I'm alarmed to say, the concern and outrage of the American people have not translated into action.

  This reticence on behalf of Christians is deeply troubling. Marriage is a sacrament designed by God that serves as a metaphor for the relationship between Christ and His Church. Tampering with His plan for the family is immoral and wrong. To violate the Lord's expressed will for humankind, especially in regard to behavior that He has prohibited, is to court disaster.

Source: http://www.nogaymarriage.com/tenarguments.asp

The article "Gay Marriage: Why Would It Affect Me?" explicitly identifies itself as argument, unlike our other examples, so it invites ideological close reading. When we ask what a text wants its reader to think or do, we come most directly to the issue of ideology. But the answer to that question is not yet quite what we mean by ideology, for remember that an ideology is a network of beliefs and attitudes. The easy answer to the question of what "Gay Marriage" wants the audience to do is that it wants to foster opposition to same-sex marriage. But that idea is part of a network of ideas, an ideology, that may be detected from a close reading of this online article.

  The ideology defended here is more complicated than simple opposition to same-sex marriage. That ideology is fundamentally a vision of the key idea of *family* and what it means to live in close, intimate, human relationships. The article presents a network of ideas in which that idea of family predominates, and the idea of opposition to same-sex marriage is actually a supporting or component part of the ideology. Argument #1 leads off, after all, with a statement about "the implications for children in a world of decaying families."

Glimpses of the centrality of family show us that opposition to same-sex marriage is seen as a contributor to the idea of family rather than as central idea in its own right. In Argument #2, the fifth paragraph closes with this result of a process of legalizing same-sex marriage: "After they [politicians and judges] have done their wretched work, the family will consist of little more than someone's interpretation of 'rights.'" This alleged destruction or immaterialization of family is the result of same-sex marriage and is offered as the reason to oppose it. The following paragraph is most revealing of this ideological kingpin, for it surveys all manner of domestic arrangements in horror ("marriage between a man and his donkey"), claiming that each such arrangement would be what a "family" would become were same-sex marriage legalized. This paragraph helps us to understand what is meant by the key ideological term *family:* it is *structure* above all.

The article argues repeatedly for a certain structure or configuration. The second paragraph of Argument #1 bemoans the statistic that "more than half of the babies born in the 1990s will spend at least part of their childhood in single-parent homes." The next paragraph foresees in horror a situation where "almost every child will have several 'moms' and 'dads,' perhaps six or eight 'grandparents,' and dozens of half-siblings." It is useful to ask about the *assumptions* the text invites the audience to make at this point. I think one central assumption is that these varying structures are to be seen in contrast to what is assumed to be the preferred arrangement: one male parent and one female parent, married, with their own biological children and only their own biological children, all living together in the same place. Notice that throughout the article, a range of living arrangements is viewed in dismay just because they all differ from that "default" structure. There is never any discussion about whether the default structure— the nuclear family, as it is sometimes called—is loving, economically nurturing, or socially supportive. The reader is to assume either that all nuclear families are nurturing and supportive or—and the article leans in this direction, I believe—that structure truly matters more than love, economics, or support.

Further evidence abounds of the nuclear family as the assumed default. Argument #5 foresees a future in which "a traditional family involving one man and one woman," a family "having a mom and a dad" will tragically not be valued more than "parents representing only one sex" or even "fatherless and motherless children" in the care of someone. The third paragraph of Argument #9 likewise envisions with horror "motherless children and fatherless kids" as the likely structural alternative to "a father and a mother." Why motherlessness and fatherlessness follow from lack of *either* a mother and a father is unclear; what is clear is that in the absence of the latter, the traditional family structure, all alternatives are horrible due to their structural flaws.

It is interesting that in terms of the evidence offered or reasons given why the reader should believe the article, religious evidence seems not to dominate. We are told that the Bible opposes nontraditional structures, but much of the evidence for that claim is secular. Only twice is the favored nuclear family structure explicitly linked to religious purposes, the first being found in Argument #9. In the first paragraph we are told, "The family has been God's primary vehicle for evangelism since the beginning." The argument continues in the next paragraph: "Its most important assignment has been the propagation of the human race and the handing down of the faith to our children." The nuclear family structure is thus seen as the instrument, perhaps the chief instrument, of the spread of religious faith. On this argument, without that structure faith would disappear. The creation of new generations and the instilling of faith in those generations are both made to depend on the family. And in Argument #10 the third paragraph argues that "[m]arriage is a sacrament designed by God that serves as a metaphor for the relationship between Christ and His Church." Again, there is no question raised as to whether the marriage is happy, contentious, bitter, long lasting, and so forth. No, the binary structure of man:woman::Christ:Church is what matters most.

The ideological centrality of family structure is further enforced by a theme running throughout "Gay Marriage," and that is that change is bad, stability is good. That assumption is entirely consistent with an ideology of structure: if your house begins to shift, you are in trouble. Expressions equating change with disaster abound. Argument #1 fears "a world where little boys and girls are shuffled from pillar to post in an ever-changing pattern of living arrangements," a world "where nothing is stable." Argument #2 argues that "legalized gay marriages will lead inexorably to polygamy," and note the irresistible change embodied in that word "inexorably." The sixth paragraph complains of legal climates that are "unstable."

Quick change is the worst. Argument #2 argues that "[i]t took less than six months" for Justice Scalia's dire prediction of change based on same-sex legal precedents to occur. Once such change begins, once same-sex marriage is approved, the third paragraph of Argument #2 tells us that "there is no place to stop" and contrasts that unstoppable change with the nuclear family's stability on "a bedrock of tradition, legal precedent, theology, and the overwhelming support of the people." Argument #3 argues that "[a]fter marriages have been redefined, divorces will be obtained instantly," and note the suddenness of such action. An image of change and movement underlies Argument #8's fear that "marriage among homosexuals will spread throughout the world." Later, that argument begs the United States to consider "where it is going," predicting that its destination is precisely to "take this step off a cliff," and note the metaphor of movement and then sudden change implied.

It is interesting that one of the calls to think or do something made by the article is directed at Christians and is found in Argument #10, second paragraph, a call to "awaken"—but what the faithful are to do when they awaken is not to move or shift but to engage in "an even greater vigil of prayer," which is a physically stable and settled position for most people. That is the sort of "action" called for in the third paragraph, not one of moving about but one of greater stillness in prayer against same-sex marriage.

An interesting shift occurs across the trajectory of the whole article when we consider the question of evidence, or what reasons the audience is given to believe what the argument asks them to believe. Early in the article, scripture or scientific studies in the past or present are cited. Specific references are sometimes not given, but what one might call "hard" evidence in support of the argument is provided. This creates a sense that the argument is well documented. As the article proceeds, however, that sort of evidence gives way to speculation about the future. The audience is seduced into a position of trusting the support for the argument; then that trust is exploited by unsupported predictions.

Argument #1 quotes "a recent article in the *Weekly Standard*" describing the state of "gay unions in Scandinavian countries" and resulting births out of wedlock. The second paragraph reports predictions based on "demographic trends" that seem reasonable enough. Paragraph 4 of Argument #1 quotes the Bible, St. Paul's letter to the Romans; it seems to be accurate and in context whether one agrees with it or not. Argument #2 continues, in its second paragraph, the trend of hard evidence, citing Supreme Court cases (*Lawrence v. Texas*) and arguments made in a Utah court. In the third paragraph legal evidence is presented from the ACLU in the Utah case.

Note the turn, then, in the sixth paragraph of Argument #2, from evidence to prediction: "Given that unstable legal climate, it is certain that some self-possessed judge, somewhere, will soon rule that three men and one woman can marry." The "evidence" has shifted from what was certainly true in the past to allegations of what must certainly be true in the future. This change in stance on the matter of evidence continues throughout the rest of the article. Argument #3 shifts to the future tense: "After marriages have been redefined, divorces will be obtained. . . . " This, of course, cannot be known as evidence because it is about the future. Argument #4 is oriented toward the future, with no recitation of past or current facts: "With the legalization of homosexual marriage, every public school in the nation will be required.." Where earlier there was evidence, now there is prediction of the future. Argument #5 is explicitly pointed toward the future: "From that point forward, courts will not be able to favor a traditional family.." Note carefully that these statements are not described in the article as prediction, and they are presented in the same level-headed, factual style with which earlier factual evidence was given. Argument #6 looks into the future: "Foster-care parents will be required.." Again, this is a prediction phrased with the calm certainty of evidence. Argument #7 is composed largely of questions that speculate on the future: "How about the impact on Social Security.." and so forth. These questions are not phrased in terms of "what if" but as if the negative consequence were a factual certainty. Argument #8 predicts that "[M]arriage among homosexuals will spread" in the future—a prediction, but not the sort of evidence with which the article began.

It is easy on one level to address the question of who is empowered and who is disempowered by the argument in this article. People not heterosexual and anyone not in a traditional nuclear family configuration are obvious candidates for disempowerment. The single parent abandoned by a spouse or who has lost a wife or husband in death would seem to be disempowered by the article as well, for they are committing the sin of nontraditional structure. People living lifestyles that require movement and change would be disempowered also, and one cannot help but wonder what the article would say of military personnel who must often move as their assignments shift. Those in traditional, nuclear families, those with stability of home life and of faith, would then be empowered. But let us consider how narrow a net that casts. An increasingly globalized economy creates increasing instability. Jobs are lost and careers are changed, often not entirely by the choice of those affected. The article thus empowers a relatively narrow sample of the population: The Stable, The Nuclear Family, The Traditional. How many among us match that description? One could say, then, that the article empowers an ideology much more than it empowers actual people. The implication is therefore that the article empowers those who would wield that ideology to obtain power over others. To empower a small priesthood, or community of those who meet a standard of morality, may in fact be the ultimate result of this article.

❖ SUMMARY AND LOOKING AHEAD

In this chapter we have studied ways in which arguments may be read closely to enable us to detect some of the ideologies they support. *Argument* was defined as *a process by which speakers and writers, together with audiences, make claims about what people should do and assemble reasons and evidence why people should do those things.* We learned that an argument faces in two directions: it tells us a speaker's ideology, and it also urges that ideology upon an audience. It is both a symptom and a creator of ideology. Arguments add up over time and space to support ideologies, and an ideology is *a systematic network of beliefs, commitments, values, and assumptions that influence how power is maintained, struggled over, and resisted.* We learned that a key attribute of ideology is that it is often *out of awareness.* One cannot fruitfully just ask people what are their networks of belief and where they got them. Ideology is most often revealed through close reading, with the guidance of several theories and methods such as Marxist theory.

Close reading of argument with a view to uncovering ideology is facilitated by asking four questions:

- What should the audience think or do?

- What must the text ask the audience to assume?

- How does the audience know what the text claims?

- Who is empowered or disempowered?

We learned that one may begin with any of these questions and that a given text will be more productively read by relying on some of these questions over others. Also, the questions merge into each other, so beginning with one leads to another.

In this book we have studied techniques of close reading. I hope that you come away from this experience knowing how to see more clearly. If you can link these techniques to theories and methods that you learn in other classes, in general reading, and in life, you can be more aware of how texts influence you. It is time now to pull these techniques together from across this book in one last close reading of a text, in the Conclusion.

Conclusion

A Close Reading Using Multiple Techniques

To view this image in full resolution, please visit www.sagepub.com/brummettstudy.

We have learned many techniques of close reading in this book—in fact, too many to use in just one reading. You should view what you have learned as a large tool kit from which you can pull many aids to close reading. But as with a real toolbox, you are likely never to use all your tools at once on a given job. So in this closing section of the book, I do not use all the tools we have discussed. Instead, I use a selection of techniques to show how different ways of reading can converge to become a complex understanding of a text. So as not to interrupt the flow of my reading, I avoid calling your attention to each particular technique or reminding you of the chapter in which each can be found, and so forth. You, the reader, must be on the lookout for my use of techniques and connect them to what you have learned. I also keep this reading as close to the level of technique as possible, not resorting to a discussion of method, much less theory. My goal in this reading is to show how a range of techniques can converge as a unified understanding of a text.

Let me also note that the reading I offer here and the techniques I use are not the only way to examine the text at hand—or any text, for that matter. You might prefer different techniques and thus discover different meanings. As long as you base your reading in solid evidence from the text disclosed through valid techniques, a variety of readings—even divergent and contradictory ones—can only deepen your understanding of texts. Let us begin.

On January 20, 2009, Barack Obama became the forty-fourth president of the United States. Two days earlier, the cartoon shown on p. 125— the syndicated *Candorville* strip, drawn by Darrin Bell—appeared in newspapers around the nation. The image—there are no words beyond those that appear on the presidential seal—is remarkably dense for a cartoon. The textual context of a daily newspaper cartoon strip usually features simple, clear drawings and a punchy joke. Each strip is meant to be taken in quickly, to produce a grin or chuckle—and then the reader moves on. This particular text is an unusual use of the medium of the comic strip in a family newspaper.

The strip of January 18 is arresting in two senses: first, because it demands that the reader stop and pay close attention if any attention is paid at all. It "arrests" you as your eyes scan the usual throwaway strips. The comic is like a puzzle asking to be solved.

Second, the strip is arresting because of how much it "says" without words, because of the heavy freight of meaning it conveys. Contrary to its usual form (and the form cartoons usually take), this strip asks the viewer to stop and consider what it shows us. For that reason, I use it as my sole textual example in this last close reading. It seems particularly designed for close reading, to call out for it. I invite you to study it, to read it carefully along with me as I apply some of the techniques we have discussed to this close reading.

Context is my main theme in this reading. Context is important in choosing techniques of close reading. It is an important influence on audiences' understandings of texts. It seems obvious that given the appearance of the cartoon two days before the inauguration of the man in the center of the strip, Barack Obama, the inauguration is part of the historical context of the text. But this idea of context is complicated, and teasing out the many nuances of context as it is invoked by the text can be rewarding.

Inaugurations fall within a specific kind of rhetorical, ceremonial genre. They are rhetorical events taking place in regularly recurring contexts. Few elements of our shared American political life are more stable than the expectation that a president will be inaugurated every four years among much pomp and circumstance and on precisely the "stage" depicted in the cartoon. The inauguration, the swearing in, and the inaugural address are highly generic and thus invoke a regularly recurring context. Expectations for how the event should proceed and what it means are recurring, although each inauguration brings its own freight of hopes and fears.

The audience brought to this inauguration an understanding that Obama is "the first African American president." That is a persona created for him in much public discourse and also by this cartoon. One could find such wording in every blog, in each television newscast and commentary, both then and now. Clearly, the text depends upon the audience's believing that this "first" is a fact and holding it as an assumption. But consider these "facts" as well: Obama is as much of European ancestry as of African. Although it is technically true to refer to him as African American—his father was African, his mother European American—he has none of the heritage of slavery and racist oppression experienced by other people called African American whose ancestors were brought to this country in chains. Although there are plenty of reports about President Obama's paternal family and ancestors in Africa, references to Obama as African *American* dominate public discourse.

It is also a "fact" that Obama's early upbringing was densely international. He was raised in the diverse and polyglot state of Hawaii and later in Indonesia, where his mother married an Indonesian man. Culturally, one might well say that Obama is neither simply African nor Kansan but instead a mix of international, cosmopolitan influences. Yet his cultural experience of the wide world is also not as commonly discussed in public conversation as is his identity as African American, and this cartoon likewise does not position Obama in that international context.

The cartoon generally reinforces the historical context of African Americans in the United States whose ancestors experienced enslavement, oppression, and discrimination. Obama is shown taking the oath of office from the late Supreme Court justice Thurgood Marshall. They are surrounded by a "cloud of witnesses" that references not the Africa of Obama's father, not the Hawaiians and Indonesians of his youth, but the enslaved Africans of the United States, ancestors of today's African Americans. Some European Americans are depicted in the cartoon, gathering around to witness and support the event. But these Whites are from the historical context of racial struggle, which invokes for purposes of argument a context of African Americans. We see John

Brown, who unsuccessfully attempted to foment a slave rebellion; Harry Truman, the president who integrated the armed forces; Dwight Eisenhower, the president who used force to integrate Central High School in Little Rock, Arkansas; and other White abolitionists and activists connected to racial struggle in this country.

A number of people of African ancestry are depicted but all within the historical context of racial struggles, slavery, and oppression in the United States: Rosa Parks, Frederick Douglass, Justice Marshall, and so forth. All of the ordinary, nameless people depicted in the cartoon are African Americans, many of them enslaved Africans in photographs from the nineteenth century. We find no ordinary European Americans, no Kansans like his mother. We find no Africans whose tradition does not channel through racism and slavery in the United States except one, and that is Obama. The text agrees with the balance of popular national discourse in ignoring that part of his history. The historical context invoked by the text firmly references Obama within the tradition of enslavement, refusal, and struggle. It removes him from his direct African history and repositions him in the context of Africans in America. The strip therefore affirms a nationwide emphasis on Obama as aligned with those whose ancestors experienced slavery in this country, even if that is contrary to his own history.

Being not literally true in any sense, the cartoon is a metaphor. The event is turned into a supernatural gathering of deceased heroes. Of course, Obama was not surrounded by these dead historical figures, so to say that he was is to produce a visual metaphor. The metaphor tells us that the inauguration, the fact of this presidency, is the confluence of a history of racial oppression and struggle and final triumph in the United States. The cartoon also makes of Obama a metonymy, reducing the abstract idea of protracted struggle and triumph into this moment of inauguration. Those who participated in that centuries-long struggle come together in the gathering imagined by the cartoon. Metaphor and metonymy ask us to see an event, an idea, within a particular context, and these tropes also support the location of Obama in a context of struggle over race and slavery in this country.

Because Obama is aligned with African Americans descended from a history of slavery and oppression, the cartoon calls to us, its readers and audience, to position ourselves within that tradition. News reports also tell us that this presidency is celebrated by the great and the ordinary internationally. People around the world find cause for applause in his international experiences. And yet you and I are not called upon by the cartoon to take up a position as citizens of the world sharing those far-flung hopes. We are called as the audience of

the strip to become personae who are also, in our dif
descendants of the struggle over race in America, whatev
heritage may be. Because that history is preeminently c
ment and opposition, of whom we are with and whom we
these alignments and oppositions are then propagated in the audience. By that I mean that we are invited to step into the particular
context being created rather than into any of the other contexts that
might be chosen. We become aware of ourselves as "enraced" within
that sad dimension of American history. We are asked to replicate the
thinking about ourselves and about America that is primarily structured around race.

Every election is a story, a narrative constructed in news reports
and commentaries, in everyday conversations among people. The historical context created by this cartoon vibrates with narrative. Each
figure depicted suggests a story. The audience is invited to look carefully for familiar faces. The cartoon is a sort of historical "Where's
Waldo?" in which we enjoy moments of recognition of the faces of
people we learned about in history books. It is up to the audience, then,
to say why that person is on the imaginary stage of the cartoon. The
cartoon is thus a visual enthymeme, a kind of argument that the audience is invited to complete. "That's Medgar Evers," we might say to
ourselves, or "There's President Johnson," and then in our own heads
we flesh out why that person is depicted. To do so, we must tell ourselves the story of each figure. We have learned these stories of the
famous in school and from television and films. For the anonymous,
ordinary, enslaved Africans we see depicted, we construct imagined
stories from the history books.

In sum, the meanings of this cartoon that I stress are the meanings
that create a context of race, slavery, oppression, and triumph in the
United States. I close this particular reading—many others are, of
course, possible—through the technique of asking about empowerment in the text. Let me shift that question somewhat to ask not which
individual or group is empowered but what way of thinking. An
agenda, a preoccupation is empowered here, which of course may have
far-reaching implications for individuals and groups.

Many elements of this text converge to insist upon the historical
context of African American enslavement and oppression in this country
as the context for President Obama's election and inauguration. We
have seen that other contexts, stories, personae, and so on that might be
called forth out of this complex event are ignored or refused. What the
text asks the audience to do, then, is to keep that context in mind as an
ongoing, recurring preoccupation. We are asked to judge actions, objects,

events, and public figures even beyond the Obama inauguration in terms of the specific context of racial oppression in this country. The text empowers an agenda, a heightened awareness of race as a context for much of what occurs and has occurred in American society.

One hears from time to time that American society or global society has gone "postracial." By this people mean that texts of popular culture, such as advertisements, film, television, and magazines, show people interacting without regard to color and that people in their everyday lives follow suit. Many commentators argue that Obama's election is itself evidence of a postracial turn.

I have been an observer of the public scene long enough to think that we are moving in that direction, although I believe we are very far from being truly postracial. In a sense there is a danger in becoming postracial or imagining that we are doing so, if remnants of racism remain. Those who think the world is postracial are more likely to be felled by racism when it occurs. So a repetition, a reinscribing of the historical context of racial struggle can serve as a call to ongoing awareness and vigilance. By insisting on this historical context of racism and the struggle of African Americans, the cartoon celebrates a step beyond that context—Obama's inauguration—at the same time that it reminds us that the context has not gone away.

But this is just my reading. Think about the techniques you have learned in this book, and return to the cartoon. What understandings will your readings yield? Onward with your reading!

References

Altheide, David L. *Media Power.* Beverly Hills: Sage, 1985. Print.

Althusser, Louis. *Lenin and Philosophy and Other Essays.* Trans. B. Brewster. New York: Monthly Review Press, 1971. Print.

Aristotle. *The Rhetoric and Poetics of Aristotle.* Trans. W. Rhys Roberts and Ingram Bywater. Ed. Edward P. J. Corbett. New York: Random House, 1954. Print. Modern Library Edition.

Aune, James Arnt. "An Historical Materialist Theory of Rhetoric." *American Communication Journal* 6 (2003): n. pag. Web. 18 May 2009. <http://acjournal .org/holdings/vol6/iss4/mcmcgee/aune.pdf>.

Black, Edwin. "The Second Persona." *Quarterly Journal of Speech* 56 (1970): 109–19. Print.

Booth, Wayne C. *A Rhetoric of Irony.* Chicago: U of Chicago P, 1974. Print.

Brummett, Barry. "A Pentadic Analysis of Ideologies in Two Gay Rights Controversies." *Central States Speech Journal* 30 (1979): 250–61. Print.

———. *Rhetorical Homologies: Form, Culture, Experience.* Tuscaloosa: U of Alabama P, 2004. Print.

———. *Rhetoric in Popular Culture.* 2nd ed. Thousand Oaks: Sage, 2006. Print.

Burke, Kenneth. *Attitudes Toward History.* 3rd ed. Berkeley: U of California P, 1984. Print.

———. *Counter-Statement.* Berkeley: U of California P, 1968. Print.

———. *A Grammar of Motives.* Berkeley: U of California P, 1962. Print.

———. *Language as Symbolic Action.* Berkeley: U of California P, 1966. Print.

———. *Permanence and Change.* Indianapolis: Bobbs-Merrill, 1965. Print.

———. *The Philosophy of Literary Form.* 3rd ed. Berkeley: U of California P, 1973. Print.

———. *A Rhetoric of Motives.* Berkeley: U of California P, 1962. Print.

———. *The Rhetoric of Religion.* Berkeley: U of California P, 1961. Print.

Campbell, Karlyn Kohrs, and Kathleen Hall Jamieson. *Form and Genre: Shaping Rhetorical Action.* Falls Church: Speech Communication Association, 1978. Print.

Cialdini, Robert B. *Influence: Science and Practice.* Boston: Allyn & Bacon, 2001. Print.

Dargis, Manohla, and A. O. Scott. "How the Movies Made a President." *New York Times.* 18 Jan. 2009: AR1. Print.

Flynn, Eileen. "Fulfilling the Spiritual Promise of a Father." *Austin American-Statesman.* 14 June 2008: F1. Print.

Goffman, Erving. *Frame Analysis.* New York: Harper Colophon, 1974. Print.

Hall, Stuart. "Signification, Representation, Ideology: Althusser and the Post-Structuralist Debates." *Critical Studies in Mass Communication* 2 (1985): 91–114. Print.

Jackson, Shirley. *The Haunting of Hill House.* New York: Popular Library, 1959. Print.

Kinneavy, James L. *A Theory of Discourse.* New York: Norton, 1971. Print.

Lacan, Jacques. *Ecrits: A Selection.* Trans. Alan Sheridan. New York: Norton, 1977. Print.

Lambert, Elizabeth. "In London, Two Historic Suites Are Reinterpreted with a Contemporary Flair." *Architectural Digest* May (2007): n. pag. Web. 29 Feb. 2008. <http://www.architecturaldigest.com/homes/hotels/2007/05/hotels_article_052007>.

McPhail, Mark Lawrence. "Ideological Criticism." *The Encyclopedia of Rhetoric and Composition: Communication from Ancient Times to the Information Age.* Ed. Theresa Enos. New York: Garland, 1996. 340–41. Print.

Perelman, Chaim, and Lucie Olbrechts-Tyteca. *The New Rhetoric: A Treatise on Argumentation.* Notre Dame: U of Notre Dame P, 1969. Print.

PETA (People for the Ethical Treatment of Animals). "Why Animal Rights?" n. pag. Web. 5 Mar. 2008. <http://www.peta.org/>.

Rubin, Rachel, and Jeffery Melnick. *Immigration and American Popular Culture.* New York: New York UP, 2006. Print.

"Sarcasm." *Merriam-Webster's Collegiate Dictionary.* 11th ed. 2006. Print.

Sciolino, Elaine. "Making Holocaust Personal to Pupils, Sarkozy Stirs Anger." *New York Times.* 16 Feb. 2008: A1, A6. Print.

Stewart-Steinberg, Suzanne. "Ideology." *The Encyclopedia of Postmodernism.* Eds. Victor E. Taylor and Charles E. Winquist. London: Routledge, 2001: 185–86. Print.

Toulmin, Stephen, Richard Rieke, and Allan Janik. *An Introduction to Reasoning.* New York: Macmillan, 1979. Print.

Woodward, Gary C., and Robert E. Denton, Jr. *Persuasion and Influence in American Life.* 5th ed. Long Grove: Waveland, 2004. Print.

Index

About the Author

Barry Brummett is the Charles Sapp Centennial Professor in Communication and Department of Communication Studies Chair at the University of Texas at Austin. He received his PhD from the University of Minnesota. Brummett has authored several articles and books, including *Rhetoric in Popular Culture* (Sage), *A Rhetoric of Style* (Southern Illinois University), and *Rhetorical Homologies: Form, Culture, Experience* (University of Alabama). He studies the rhetoric of popular culture and the theories of Kenneth Burke.

Supporting researchers for more than 40 years

Research methods have always been at the core of SAGE's publishing program. Founder Sara Miller McCune published SAGE's first methods book, *Public Policy Evaluation*, in 1970. Soon after, she launched the *Quantitative Applications in the Social Sciences* series—affectionately known as the "little green books."

Always at the forefront of developing and supporting new approaches in methods, SAGE published early groundbreaking texts and journals in the fields of qualitative methods and evaluation.

Today, more than 40 years and two million little green books later, SAGE continues to push the boundaries with a growing list of more than 1,200 research methods books, journals, and reference works across the social, behavioral, and health sciences. Its imprints—Pine Forge Press, home of innovative textbooks in sociology, and Corwin, publisher of PreK–12 resources for teachers and administrators—broaden SAGE's range of offerings in methods. SAGE further extended its impact in 2008 when it acquired CQ Press and its best-selling and highly respected political science research methods list.

From qualitative, quantitative, and mixed methods to evaluation, SAGE is the essential resource for academics and practitioners looking for the latest methods by leading scholars.

For more information, visit **www.sagepub.com**.